TRIAL BY JURY

A Trial Lawyer Recounts His Favorite Courtroom Battles

Lawrence Rookhuyzen

BookLocker

Saint Petersburg, Florida

DEDICATION

Jury service is one of the highest forms of civic duty we can perform as private citizens. This book is dedicated to the men and women, who when summoned, faithfully respond and serve. Without them—there would be no jury trials.

ACKNOWLEDGMENTS

Editing assistance by Conan Grames
Formatting assistance by helberta@fiverr.com
Cover design by graphixdesignax.com

DISCLAIMER

This non-fiction work is the author's recollection of real people and events. He has related those facts to the best of his knowledge. The author understands that the recollection of the same events by others may differ from his own. If there is distortion, he is not only open, but eager, for correction.

The author has not intended in any way to distress, insult, defame, embarrass, and or invade the privacy of any person mentioned. The opinions expressed herein are those of the author.

Hemingway once said that for him there was only one way to account for things—to tell the whole truth about them, holding back nothing; tell the reader the way it truly happened; the ecstasy and sorrow, remorse, and how the weather was, and, with any luck, the reader will find his or her way to the heart of the thing itself.

This is what the author has tried to do.

CONTENTS

PREFACE

Very few civil lawyers see the inside of a courtroom during their first years of practice—let alone try any cases. But fresh out of law school I was hired by a civil litigation firm and thrust into my first superior court jury trial. I soon discovered that success comes through trial and error. As I progressed from one case to the next, I learned a lot about myself, my clients, opposing lawyers, the judges, and more importantly—the jurors.

This book contains the non-fictional accounts of twenty-two jury trials involving real people and real events. Each chapter provides a snapshot in time of a different lawsuit and depicts what it was like to be a young trial lawyer learning the ropes and survive in an adversarial environment.

These cases chronicle several of the invaluable lessons learned in and out of the courtroom. Hopefully my real-life experiences will instill in the reader a greater appreciation and respect for the American jury system.

With time passing and memory dimming, I felt an obligation to preserve and share a few of my trial successes and failures.

After reviewing the court files, my trial notes, and verdict publications, the words started flowing out of my head and onto the paper; my memory came alive and I was truly reliving these jury trials as if they had occurred yesterday.

The following pages contain some of the thrilling victories and agonizing defeats that helped shaped my legal career.

Lawrence Rookhuyzen
Southern California, 2019

What is a jury trial?

A jury trial, or trial by jury, is a legal proceeding in which a group of private citizens listen to evidence and then make a decision. It is distinguished from a bench trial in which a judge makes all decisions.

Where did it come from?

The right to trial by jury in United States law, is one of the most time-honored inheritances from England's Magna Carta that refers to the guarantee that courts will depend on a body of citizens to render judgments in most civil and criminal cases. The Magna Carta's political intent—to prevent the king's domination of the courts—inspired later generations to view the right to a trial by jury as one of the basic safeguards of freedom from an arbitrary government.

Eighteenth-century Americans viewed the right to a jury trial as one of the essential liberties of a free country. And although the United States Constitution recognized a right to a jury trial in criminal cases, the states demanded a constitutional amendment to guarantee a jury trial in civil cases as well, leading to the creation of the Seventh Amendment.

One

Beginner's Luck

Connolly v. Webb (OCSC-Santa Ana/Verdict 8/6/1985)

Not long after joining the Orange County office of McKay Byrne Graham & Van Dam, a Los Angeles based civil litigation defense firm, I was thrust into my first Superior Court jury trial. I'll admit I was wet behind the ears and didn't know what I was doing—but I was ambitious and didn't fear anything—except failure.

Connolly arose out of an automobile versus pedestrian accident near the Orange County-John Wayne Airport. The plaintiff, James Connolly, was a forty-year-old welding supply salesman. He jaywalked across Campus Boulevard and stepped up onto the landscaped center divider. Then he stepped out onto Airport Way South—directly into the path of defendant Daniel Webb's oncoming vehicle. As a result of the collision, Connolly suffered injury to his left knee collateral ligament with on-going residual complaints.

"Pedestrians always have the right-of-way" is an idiom most of us are acquainted with, but I soon discovered there are exceptions to the rule.

The plaintiff's attorney John W. Busby sued Mr. Webb contending he was speeding. He also sued the County of Orange claiming the location of the accident constituted a dangerous condition of public property and contended the County should have provided a marked crosswalk. Eric Bluemke, another young attorney, represented the County.

Occasionally, we defense lawyers get a break. In this case, the Highway Patrol—Traffic Collision Investigation Report identified an eyewitness. Unfortunately, in the four years between the accident and the trial date, the witness had moved. We located him living near Springfield, Missouri, where he was working as a dairy farmer. Because there was no one else to milk the cows, he was unavailable to travel to California for trial.

This is when I learned to appreciate the power of witness *depositions*. Depositions are oral statements taken out of court and under oath to perpetuate testimony of a witness who may be unavailable for trial. The eyewitness agreed to be deposed at his rural dairy farm.

The day before the deposition, I flew to Springfield. By the time we finally touched down, I'd changed planes twice and crossed two time zones. I was tired. At the small airport, I grabbed the last rental car, a big Lincoln Town Car (I was used to driving a small BMW 318i). By this time, it was getting late, and I was eager to get to my hotel.

Somehow I managed to miss the only exit into town and I drove for miles without seeing another off-ramp or even an area to turn around. The later it got, the harder I pressed the gas pedal. Suddenly, in my rearview mirror, I saw the flashing red, white, and blue lights coming from one of Missouri's finest.

When the officer came up to my car door, he reminded me of Sheriff Buford T. Justice in Burt Reynold's *Smokey and the Bandit* movies, complete with a Smokey-the-Bear hat and heavy Southern drawl. After showing him my California driver's license, he asked me what I was doing so far from home. I hesitated telling him I was an attorney—but I had learned the hard way that honesty is always the best policy. I confessed this was my first time visiting his fair state, I was there on business, I'd missed the turn-off into Springfield, and could he give me directions.

I'll never forget his response: "Well now sonny, I can give you directions to town, but it might be on the back of this here ticket." He then retreated to his patrol car for what seemed like an eternity. When he came back, he asked me, "If I write you this ticket, you, being an attorney and all, you would probably represent yourself?" I replied, "Yes, sir." He then said, "I'm going to let you off with a warning—but I'm going to follow you back to town." I thanked him profusely.

Mr. Busby did not make the trip out to Missouri, but instead hired a local attorney to attend the witness deposition in his place. The next morning, the local guy called and offered me a ride out to the deposition location, assuring me I would never find the address on my own. Call it *Southern hospitality*. He was right. The dairy farm was off the interstate at the end of an unmarked dirt road—way out in the tulies[1].

The deposition went forward as scheduled. The eyewitness confirmed that Mr. Connolly *did not* check for cross traffic before stepping off the center median and

---

[1] The "Tulies" is defined in *Word Origins* as meaning the same thing as "out-in-the-boondocks" or "in-the-middle-of-no-where."

into the path of Mr. Webb's oncoming vehicle.

At trial, I had my paralegal take the stand and read the eyewitness's exculpatory testimony from his deposition transcript.

Unfazed, Mr. Busby asked the jury to award his client $393,000. I was sweating bullets while the jury deliberated, but after a seven day trial, the jurors found my client and the County—not liable. They specifically found Mr. Webb was traveling within the posted speed limit and had no opportunity to avoid the accident.

Our case was tried in the Orange County Superior Court-Santa Ana, before Judge Richard N. Parslow, Jr., a former police officer.

Back at the office, my boss, John McKay, was pleased with the verdict, as was our client's insurance carrier, who wrote a nice note to the partners:

"Gentlemen: Thank you for the most refreshing news we've had in a long time. It is nice to know that we can still win meritless lawsuits. I want to personally thank Mr. Rookhuyzen for a job well done. He was well prepared and as a result the evidence was put in a perspective most favorable to our client. Mr. Rookhuyzen's professionalism and dedication to his job, reflects the quality of work which is always appreciated in our business."

My fifteen minutes of fame only whetted my appetite and I couldn't wait to get back in the courtroom.

Two

Anything Can Happen

Schaefer v. Tindall Trucking (SDSC-Escondido/Verdict 8/10/1987)

I just assumed all my future jury trials would proceed as smoothly as my first, but I was soon dissuaded from that assumption. *Schaefer v. Tindall Trucking* was a big wake-up call.

First, I had not one—but two—Type A personality, former San Diego Deputy District Attorneys, David Ronquillo and Terry Singleton, tag-teaming against me throughout the trial. Second, the trial was held in their backyard—Escondido. Third, their strategy was to intimidate a young and inexperienced defense attorney— so I would just give up and throw in the towel. And fourth, as if that wasn't enough, our truck driver James Brownlow had moved out-of-state without leaving a forwarding address and we were unable to locate him in time for trial.

The plaintiff, Jeanne Schaefer, a twenty-eight-year-old, electronics assembler for NCR in Rancho Bernardo, contended, while on her lunch break, she was operating her Chevrolet Blazer in a proper manner, when the defendant's driver made an illegal U-turn in front of her. She claimed she was unable to avoid colliding with the big rig.

Schaefer sustained a non-displaced fracture of the right thumb, fracture of the pelvis and sacrococcygeal junction, plus low back pain. Her attorneys were so confident the case was going their way, they asked the jury to award her $453,000—even though before trial their demand was a paltry $250,000.

I explained to the jurors Ms. Schaefer was exceeding the speed limit and had she been attentive, she would have been able to see the defendant's rig for at least two-hundred-seventy feet before impact. This gave the plaintiff plenty of time and distance to bring her vehicle to a stop without a collision. Instead, she chose to try to drive around the front of Mr. Brownlow's turning tractor-trailer rig. Therefore, it was *Schaefer* who caused the accident—and not the driver of the eighteen-wheeler.

My accident reconstruction and medical experts did

not hold up well under the pounding cross-examination of the plaintiff's attorneys. Even worse, since our truck driver was unavailable, there was no one to rebut Schaefer's testimony.

Just when I thought all was lost and ready to give up, I solicited some unexpected testimony from the on-scene investigating traffic officer. During his inspection of Schaefer's vehicle, he found *Marijuana debris* in the ash tray. (In those days—that was a big *no-no*). Both plaintiff attorneys jumped up out of their seats objecting loudly, but the judge overruled their objections, and allowed the police officer's testimony into evidence. For the first time in the trial, I saw a glimmer of hope.

The next day, the plaintiff came up with an alibi that the *weed-in-the-ash-tray* was left there by one of her friends. But the jurors heard the officer's testimony; the damage was done. This case was tried in the San Diego County Superior Court-Escondido before the Honorable Harley Earwicker.

Despite non-stop harassment from opposing counsel, and the other disadvantages I faced defending this action, my efforts were rewarded when the jury returned a verdict for my client.

After the court clerk read the decision, I was still in a state of euphoria and didn't notice Schaefer's attorneys leave the courtroom. Later, Mrs. Tindall commented to me that they must have crawled out—*underneath* the carpet.

A lesson learned from this case: Never under estimate the jury or give up even when everything seems to be going in the wrong direction, since anything can happen during trial.

This case also taught me not to take opposing counsel's harassment personally—because *winning* is always a trial lawyer's sweetest revenge.

Post-trial: A few years later, the State Bar Magazine reported that attorney Ronquillo was *suspended* in 2004 and subsequently *disbarred* in 2010 for engaging in acts of moral turpitude, dishonesty or corruption, and misappropriating client funds with a record of prior discipline.

Three

A Sudden Shift in Momentum

*Bowen v. Kerstin-Laguna Beach, Inc., et al. (OCSC-Santa Ana/
Verdict 2/22/1988)*

Bowen v. Kerstin was a particularly memorable trial. My opposing counsel, Marjorie Day, was by far, the most well-known and successful female trial lawyer in Orange County; a real legend. I was going up against one of the best.

Boy, was she smooth. During jury selection, she coyly asked the jurors, "Would you hold Mr. Rookhuyzen's 'glowing youth' against me?" and "Does anyone think I should be home baking cookies for my grandchildren?"

The case was set before Superior Court Judge James R. Ross. A bit of a character himself, Ross traced his roots back to Jesse James; and had even authored a book about the outlaw. As a lawyer, Ross had made a name for himself as a plaintiff's personal injury attorney. On the bench, he could be crotchety. For example, if a lawyer objected to his demeanor or his courtroom rules, Ross would proudly inform them, "I've been appealed on this issue before, but never overturned."

My client, Kerstin Florian, was a native of Sweden, and the owner and president of Kerstin-Laguna Beach, Inc., an international skin care products company. She also operated a Swedish massage and skin care salon in one of that city's finer resort hotels.

The plaintiff, Margaret Bowen, while visiting from Boulder, Colorado, had gone to Kerstin's salon to get a full-body, deep-muscle, Swedish massage. Bowen claimed during the massage, her head had been forcefully rotated, causing instability in the vertebrae of her neck, that later required her to undergo surgery.

As I've mentioned before, sometimes defense attorneys get a break. In this trial, I needed every break I could get. Since Ms. Bowen lived in Colorado, all her medical treatment had taken place there.

Her primary care doctor, orthopedic surgeon Courtney Brown, M.D., practiced in Denver. As the trial date approached, we learned Dr. Brown was a physician for the U.S. Olympic ski team, and therefore, would not be available to attend trial during the winter games. For this reason, Marjorie arranged for the doctor's deposition to be videotaped at his office.

Although videotaped depositions were not unusual in 1988, smaller law firms did not use them on a regular basis, because of the additional expense. Obviously, Marjorie believed this doctor's testimony warranted the extra cost.

It had been snowing steady for three days before I arrived in Denver to attend the deposition; just driving to the doctor's office was an adventure. When I arrived, Marjorie was already there. We were informed the doctor was still at the hospital, the deposition would be delayed at least an hour, and then ushered into a conference room. After I read every magazine in the room twice, and the wait far exceeded an hour, Dr. Brown opened the door and came striding into the room muttering "This is a damn inconvenience to me."

Really? A damn inconvenience to *him*? I had traveled to Colorado in the middle-of-the-winter and driven to his office through three feet of snow for *his* convenience. Then I realized—this was Marjorie's problem—not mine. She quickly asked to speak with the doctor in private. It gets better. The deposition went forward and a few days later a copy of the videotape arrived in the mail. When we played the video tape—there was nothing on it but fuzzy white lines across the screen.

Our case was called to start trial during the 1988 Winter Olympics and Marjorie had no opportunity to re-tape the doctor's deposition. This experience taught me a big lesson—always make sure your audio-visual equipment is working properly.

However, the most memorable event in the trial occurred during the jury selection process called—*voir dire*.[2] Judge Ross, in a condescending tone, inquired of the jurors, "By a show of hands, have any of you been to *Mr. Rookhuyzen's* massage parlor?" (I didn't know I owned a massage parlor). All I could do was bite my tongue and stare down at my shoelaces.

When I eventually looked up, I noticed one of the prospective jurors, an attractive brunette sitting in the front row of the jury box, had her hand in the air. I was stunned. Everybody was. You could have heard a pin drop. What were the chances that someone on this jury panel had been to my client's salon for a massage?

This was a make-or-break moment for my case. When Judge Ross finally got around to asking this young

---

[2] *Voir Dire* (Old French for "to speak the truth") is defined by *Black's Law Dictionary* as the preliminary examination of a witness or juror.

lady if she had gone to my client's salon for a massage—she replied very credibly, "Yes"—she had been there. "Yes"—she had gotten the same deep-muscle Swedish massage that the plaintiff claimed to have gotten. "Yes"—she had loved it and would go back again anytime. You could tell the men in the jury box were eating this up. This beauty had their full attention.

The young woman's responses to the judge's questions had the effect of turning night into day and bitter into sweet. We could not have asked for a better endorsement.

What a way to start a trial. In just a few minutes we went from Judge Ross's sleazy insinuation of "Mr. Rookhuyzen's massage parlor"—to this gorgeous gal's description of a first-class establishment—complete with a *Good Housekeeping* seal of approval. Yes—indeed, momentum in a courtroom can shift that quickly.

When it was my turn to question her, I posed the same questions Judge Ross asked, just in case anyone in the jury pool had not been listening.

Believe me, Marjorie Day could not wait to use one of her *peremptory challenges*[3] to get rid of this prospective

---

[3] A *Peremptory Challenge* is a right each party has during jury selection to dismiss a prospective juror without having to state the reason.

juror. But it was too late; the bell had been rung—and you can't unring a bell.

During the trial, our orthopedic expert, Dr. Michael Abdala, explained to the jury that plaintiff had a well-documented medical history of pre-existing neck injury. That history included a motor vehicle accident just two weeks before the massage, which had aggravated her nagging neck problems going back to November 1981. Her injuries, he testified, had come from the whiplash in the auto accident, falls while skiing, and playing tennis four-days-a-week; and not from any single manipulation during the massage.

Like the pro she was, Marjorie Day just smiled at the jury and asked them nicely to award her client half-a-million dollars for all her troubles.

But instead, after a six day trial, the jury returned a verdict for the defense.

This trial taught me to keep faith in the jury system. Faith that the truth will eventually come out and set you free. Faith that God will give you the strength and courage to hang on and not give up. But most of all, it taught me something very important—patience.

Post-trial: Beating a living legend like Marjorie Day on her own turf was priceless. It also helped to increase

my reputation as a trial lawyer in the legal community—
something money can't buy.

Four

No Duty to Inspect

Martin v. Johnson Trucking (OCSC-NB Harbor/Verdict 7/18/1988)

My next case involved a thirty-seven-year-old warehouseman, Charles W. Martin, who was unloading an overseas shipping container with a forklift, when a portion of the container's wooden floor caved-in, causing him to fall off. As a result, he injured the vertebrae in his cervical spine resulting in residual neck and shoulder pain, loss of grip, and emotional problems.

My client, the defendant, Johnson Trucking, had been hired to pick up the subject cargo container from the docks in Long Beach and transport it to the warehouse where plaintiff Martin was working. Thus, the trucking company did not own or load the container.

The plaintiff's attorney contended that the defendant

had a duty to inspect the container's floor. We contended the company had no such duty to inspect because Johnson Trucking was hired only to transport the container from the docks to the warehouse, not to insure its contents or the condition. Moreover, even if such a duty existed, the defect in the floor could not have been readily discovered by a reasonable inspection. (See: *Garner v. Pacific Electric Railway Co.* (1962) 202 C.A. 2d 720).

Accordingly, liability for the accident must rest solely with the owner of the shipping container—U.S. Lines—whom Plaintiff failed to name in his lawsuit.

The proceedings were long and drawn out, primarily because the case had the potential for a large damage recovery. For that reason, Martin's attorney felt the need to impress the jury by calling a lot of witnesses and introducing a ton of exhibits to support his injury and money damage claims.

In trial, sometimes *more* is not always better. Martin's attorney, Robert Kaplan, called several expert witnesses, including a neurologist, an orthopedist, a vocational rehabilitation specialist, an economist, and an insurance claims adjuster.

During Mr. Kaplan's closing argument, I have to admit, I almost panicked when he asked the jury to award Mr. Martin $592,000. The case was tried in the Orange County Superior Court-Newport Beach Harbor before the Honorable Robert C. Todd—a very good trial judge.

After eleven long days of testimony, an exhausted and dreary-eyed jury followed my arguments, rejected the plaintiff's contentions, and returned a verdict for the defense.

There is an old trial lawyer's proverb that goes something like this: "If the facts are against you, argue the law. If the law is against you, argue the facts. If both the facts and the law are against you, pound on the table and yell."

This case taught me that it always helps to have the *facts* and the *law* on your side.

Five

Hometowned in San Diego

Larson v. Loyd, et. al. (SDSC-Central/Verdict 1/18/1989)

Larson v. Loyd arose out of a collision between an eighteen-wheel tractor-trailer rig and a pickup truck on a busy San Diego freeway off-ramp. The plaintiff, Kurt Larson, age sixteen, had only been licensed to drive for four months. At the time of the accident, Larson and a friend were on their way to the beach. He was driving his father's pickup truck southbound on the I-15 freeway near the Charger's football stadium.

My client, Michael Loyd, was driving his sixty-five-foot tractor with two empty haul-trailers home from a work site at the corner of Friars Road and Zion.

Both vehicles were in the exit-lane at the same time. Larson contended that Loyd illegally changed lanes and forced Larson's pickup truck into the concrete barrier on the west side of the exit-ramp, causing the pickup to go airborne, flip over, and land on its roof. My accident reconstruction expert testified, based on the physical evidence, the accident could not have happened as described by the plaintiff.

Larson suffered a torn meniscus injury to his knee. His passenger sustained no injuries.

I contended Mr. Loyd's rig entered the I-15 South at Friar's Road and remained in the lane which turns into the off-ramp lane for 8 West—thus, Loyd had no reason to change lanes. I also asserted Larson attempted to pass Loyd's rig on the shoulder, but ran out of room to pass safely.

During this trial, I found out what it meant to get *hometowned*[4]. The plaintiff's counsel, Dale Larabee, was a well-known local attorney in the San Diego community. This case was tried in the downtown San Diego Superior Court. Our judge, Carlos Cazares, mentioned several times in my presence that he knew and liked Larabee.

This bias was demonstrated time-after-time in the evidentiary rulings the judge made during the trial. For

---

[4] *Hometowned* is defined in *Nolo's Plain English Law Dictionary* as "slang for a lawyer or client suffering discrimination by a judge who seems to favor locals over out-of-towners."

example, California Highway Patrol officers are *not* accident reconstruction experts and their testimony is routinely limited to their traffic collision report. During trial, however, the court over my strenuous objection, allowed the CHP officer, who had no background or training in forensic accident reconstruction, to testify as an expert on the *cause* of the accident. When I made repeated objections or requested a side bar, the judge would cut me off or deny my request, preventing me from making a record for appeal.

This is not how our legal system is supposed to work. Judges, like attorneys, must follow strict rules of professional conduct. In my humble opinion, as a result of the court's lack of impartiality, my client did not receive a fair trial.

In his closing argument, attorney Larabee asked the jury to award his client $500,000. I wasn't surprised when the jury returned a verdict for the plaintiff—fortunately for us—it was in a lesser amount of $175,000.

In a small victory for the defense, the jury found young Mr. Larson to be thirty-five percent at fault for the accident. As a result, under comparative negligence principles, his recovery was reduced to $113,750. Still, I felt that was a lot of money in 1989 for a torn meniscus injury.

Post-trial: Had the verdict been larger, we might have filed an appeal based on judicial irregularities. Looking back now, I can see why defense attorneys in civil trials, almost always request a *jury* to prevent getting *hometowned*. Had I waived a jury and gone with a bench trial; judge Cazares probably would have awarded plaintiff the total amount of damages requested by attorney Larabee—without assessing any comparative fault to Larson.

The decision to demand a jury trial in this case saved my client the difference between $500,000 and $113,750. Thank goodness for juries.

Six

David and Goliath

Myers v. Southern California Edison, Cotter's Tree Service and Frank/Sheila Hanrahan (OCSC-Santa Ana/Verdict 4/10/1989)

Wrongful death cases, by definition, are always sad. This one involved the death of a fifteen-year-old teenager who climbed to the top of a neighbor's sixty-foot tall Monterey pine, lost his balance, came in contact with an Edison high-voltage overhead power line and electrocuted. The plaintiff Nancy Myers was the boy's mother. She was represented in the action by a well-known L.A. super law firm Girardi Keese and Crane.

Edison was defended by an experienced trial attorney William Falkenhainer. I represented Cotter's Tree Service, a family owned and operated business, hired by Edison to trim the tree in question. The homeowners, Frank and Sheila Hanrahan, were represented by another young defense lawyer, Peter Simpson.

Plaintiff Myers contended all three defendants were negligent, alleging Edison did not follow their own line clearance tree guidelines; Cotter's Tree Service didn't follow Edison's guidelines; and the Hanrahans should have prevented the boy from climbing the tree.

Robert Keese, one of his firm's senior partners, tried the case for the plaintiff. It was fun and educational to watch the two older and more experienced lawyers, Keese and Falkenhainer, verbally sparing with each other. I vividly remember Bill Falkenhainer begin his closing argument by stating to the jury: "Mr. Keese is a really, really good attorney (When he said that I just about fell out of my chair. It's not what I expected Bill to say. Besides, I didn't think Keese was *really* that good. But, Bill continued on) in fact, he (Keese) is so good, that he is able to put words into the mouths of the witnesses." I had to smile at that backhanded compliment.

The homeowners sat through the entire eight-day trial. Mrs. Hanrahan was very emotional and the jury could see she shared the plaintiff's loss. Her children had been best friends with the decedent. In comparison, the plaintiff Nancy Myers was less emotional and more stoic;

I think the jurors noticed that also.

The trial was covered by beat reporters from the *Los Angeles Times* and the *Orange Coast Daily Pilot*. Not being media savvy in those days, when interviewed, I requested they not mention my client, fearing negative publicity might hurt their business.

This case was tried before the Honorable James L. Smith in the Orange County Superior Court-Santa Ana. During my third year of law school, I had taken Judge Smith's *Trial Advocacy* course. He was one of the first judges, at least in Orange County, to keep trial notes on his computer and be hooked up in real time to the court reporter.

At the end of Mr. Keese's emotionally charged closing argument, he asked the jury to award Ms. Myers $1.5 million. That made me very nervous.

After eight days of trial, the jury, although sympathetic, rejected plaintiff's arguments, and to our relief, found all defendants—not liable.

This was a tragic accident and we all felt deep sympathy for Ms. Myers, but none of the defendants were *legally* responsible for her son's death. There are accidents where no one is at fault.

Post-trial: My faith in the jury system continued to grow; and despite overwhelming sympathy for the plaintiff—the jury was able to put their emotions aside and base their verdict on the facts and the law.

At trial—we had battled the legal equivalent of *Goliath* (1 Samuel 17) in the Girardi Keese & Crane firm—and won. Even super-lawyers lose cases once in a while.

Seven

Slip and Fall

Verstegen v. Phoenix Club, Inc. (OCSC-Santa Ana/Verdict 1/18/1990)

The opposing counsel in my next trial was George A. Peters Jr., an Orange County criminal defense attorney. I don't believe he had any previous *civil* trial experience, nevertheless, I knew criminal defense attorneys had to be quick on their feet, and should never be underestimated.

George was easy to get along with. He told me once when his *criminal* clients didn't like the outcome of their case, they had no qualms about driving by and shooting a few bullets at his house to express their displeasure. That reaffirmed to me I had chosen the correct field of law —*civil* litigation.

This accident case arose out of a slip and fall on the

dance floor of the Phoenix Club, a popular German themed restaurant/bar in Anaheim.

Barbara Alice Verstegen, was a personable, fifty-one-year-old, single, English lady, who worked as a paralegal for the State Bar. After work she liked to go *Swing Dancing* at the Phoenix Club.

On the night in question, she and her partner were dancing *swing.* When she spun out, she slipped and fell on what she believed was a slick spot on the floor. Alice cracked the upper-end of her femur requiring Neufeld pins. Unfortunately, due to necrosis, Ms. Verstegen had to undergo a complete hip replacement. Her dancing days were over.

This case introduced me to the wide world of slip and fall accidents. People slip and fall everywhere. At home. At work. At the grocery store. On public sidewalks. Just about anywhere. There is no end to people slipping and falling.

Notwithstanding the fact many plaintiff personal injury attorneys make a good living off these types of cases, the majority of those that do go to trial, get defensed. This is due in large part because most jurors still believe you should look where you are walking—or in this case—dancing. And, unless there is a big oil spill or banana peel involved, if you fall, it's usually your fault.

This case should have settled before trial. The plaintiff initially demanded $300,000. Later she reduced her demand to $200,000; and finally to $140,000. At trial however, she asked the jury to award her $250,000.

Even though before trial we had offered Alice a generous $55,000 to settle this questionable liability case, I still advised my client's insurance company that they should consider *increasing* their settlement offer to limit their risk exposure. With such a likeable plaintiff and serious injury, this case had a potentially high damage risk. But, instead of following my advice, the claims representative just pointed to my reputation for getting defense verdicts and refused to increase the offer. This is what we call putting *unnecessary* pressure on your trial counsel.

During the presentation of the defendant's case, I introduced evidence showing at the time she fell, Ms. Verstegen had consumed two *Tom Collins*, was dancing fast with an aggressive dance partner who spun her out; and those factors combined to cause her to lose her balance.

I was also able to produce evidence that maintenance of the dance floor was not the problem. In fact, no one that night reported a slick spot; and the plaintiff left the

Club without notifying management about the fall.

Ms. Verstegen's dance partner was hard to track down, but we finally found him residing in Nevada. A few weeks before starting the trial, I traveled to Reno and took his deposition. The testimony of this witness could not have been more favorable. He testified: "There was nothing wrong with the dance floor;" "It's the best dance floor in Orange County;" and "Plaintiff was just dancing fast, lost her balance, and fell."

Once again, locating and deposing a percipient witness to the incident with testimony favorable to our case, proved to be the key to a winning defense.

After a five day trial, the jury returned a verdict in favor of the Phoenix Club. This case was tried in the Orange County Superior Court-Santa Ana before the Honorable Claude Owens.

Post-trial: After the case was over, I received a congratulatory letter from both my client and the opposing attorney on behalf of Ms. Verstegen. Let me assure you that didn't happen very often.

This case will always remind me that the practice of law is, and always should be, a *civil* profession.

Eight

A Reversal of Fortune

Lundgren dba CWI Car Co. v. Occidental F&C Co. of North Carolina, et. al. (OCSC-Santa Ana/Verdict 4/4/1990)

During the late 1980s and early 1990s, first- and third-party Insurance Bad Faith lawsuits were sweeping the state and all the rage with the plaintiffs' bar. Juries were returning huge damage verdicts against insurance companies for alleged *bad faith* handling of insurance claims.

In June 1983, the plaintiff Ed Lundgren, doing business as, CWI Car Co., was a used car dealer who purchased an Automobile Dealership and Garage Owners Liability Insurance Policy from my client—defendant (1) Occidental Fire & Casualty Co. of North Carolina—through a wholesale broker defendant (2)

Parvin Ins. Brokers. The retail insurance broker was defendant (3) Henaman-Werdell, Inc. and the premium finance company was defendant (4) Tifco, Inc. Each defendant had separate legal counsel. Even I needed a score card to keep all the various defendants, their attorneys, and legal contentions straight.

In August 1983, the plaintiff's insurance policy was cancelled because of the poor driving records of Lundgren and his business partner. On August 11, 1983, Occidental mailed the plaintiff a certified notice of cancellation effective August 24, 1983.

Nevertheless, the plaintiff continued to pay Tifco under the insurance finance agreement. In June 1984, the plaintiff incurred property damage on two of its used cars and submitted claims. Defendant Occidental denied those claims based on the policy cancellation.

The plaintiff attorney, Mark R. Schwartz, filed suit against the above-named players claiming that Lundgren never received notice of the policy cancellation and continued to pay Tifco under the premium finance agreement.

Attorney Schwartz argued because the plaintiff continued to make the premium payments, that fact supported the claim he never received the cancellation notice. Therefore, the defendants were liable for breach of contract, negligence, fraud, tortious refusal to provide insurance and pay claims while wrongly accepting premiums, plus intentional infliction of emotional distress. Defendant Tifco returned the *unearned* premium payments to the plaintiff before trial started.

The case was ordered to mandatory, judicial, non-binding arbitration; but the hearing was a farce. The defendant parties submitted written legal briefs, but the arbitrator, *without* reading them or holding any witness examination or discussion—issued a $5 million-dollar award for the plaintiff.

All defendants requested Trial De Novo[5] effectively vacating the seven-figure arbitration award and setting the case back on the court's civil trial calendar.

The case went forward in the Orange County Superior Court-Santa Ana before a recently appointed jurist and former Federal prosecutor Nancy Wieben Stock.

Due to the number of parties, lawyers, witnesses, and documentary evidence, the proceedings consumed ten court days.

---

[5] *Request for Trial De Novo* is an option either party has following a court ordered non-binding arbitration. If one side or the other disagrees with the arbitrator's award they can file the *Request* and the award is nullified and vacated (set aside) by the court.

During trial, I realized that in order to authenticate our *smoking gun*, we needed the person who mailed out the certified notice of cancellation to come into court and so testify. Without such a witness, we could not raise the necessary legal presumption that supported our defense—that the cancellation notice had been properly mailed out in the normal course of business.

By 1990, almost seven years had passed since the mailing of the cancellation notice. We discovered that Occidental's former local agent, Rose Kyger, the person who had prepared and mailed out the cancellation notice, was no longer with the company. Visions of disgruntled ex-employees kept swirling in my head.

After considerable effort, I finally located an address for Rose in Orange County. I drove to her house, parked my car, knocked on the door, took a deep breath, and begged for her help. When Ms. Kyger testified in court that she had prepared and mailed out the cancellation notice to plaintiff in the usual course of business, her testimony literally sucked-the-wind-out of the plaintiff's case.

One of my partners, Jim Van Dam, was fond of saying, "I'd rather be lucky than good any day." Yes, but it's best to be both. I also acknowledge luck is often due to good people like Rose Kyger.

After their deliberations, the jury returned a *unanimous* verdict for all defendants. The jurors' decision resulted in one of the largest post-arbitration *reversals of fortune* in civil trial history. Plaintiff Lundgren went from a $5 million-dollar arbitration award to zip-zero-nada at trial.

Post-trial: A take away from this case was that when multiple defendants are represented by separate counsel, and their interests are joined against the Plaintiff, they should work together, and not against each other.

After the defense verdict, the plaintiff attorney confided to all counsel that his client had not been totally *candid* with him about receiving the cancellation notice.

Nine

You Can't Win 'em All

Young v. Marcello Trucking (LASC-Long Beach/Verdict 5/7/1990)

Due to certain demographics and other social-economic factors, some civil court jurisdictions are not friendly to defendants. The Los Angeles Superior Court-Long Beach is one of those jurisdictions where jurors seem to favor injured workers no matter who is at fault. This case taught me an all-important, but still humbling lesson—*you can't win 'em all.*

The plaintiff, Kathleen Ann Young, was a longshoreman—marine dock clerk. She claimed while standing on a wooden pallet in the warehouse doing paper work, an employee of defendant Marcello Trucking, without warning bumped into her pallet with a forklift. This caused her to lose her balance and strike her knee, which she had injured in a motor vehicle accident earlier that year.

Marcello's employee contended he verbally warned Ms. Young that he might bump the pallet she was standing on because of the limited area in which he had to maneuver the forklift. I argued, therefore, our employee could not be negligent, because plaintiff Young had *assumed-the-risk* of injury by choosing to remain on top of the pallet after being warned.

Plaintiff's attorney, James T. Perona, was a senior partner, in the well-known Long Beach personal injury firm of Perona, Langer, LaTorraca & Beck. He felt at home in the Long Beach courthouse and knew the damage juries there could inflict upon unsuspecting defendants.

Consequently, Perona was confident when he asked the jurors to award his client $750,000, even though his pre-trial demand was only $250,000, and Marcello Trucking's settlement offer was $150,000.

The trial consumed six days and the jury awarded Plaintiff Young $380,000. It was a relief this amount was about half of the $750,000 figure requested by attorney Perona—but nonetheless, the verdict was still a shock to one not familiar with Long Beach juries.

In my opinion, if this same case had been tried in

Orange county—I'm sure we would have won it nine-out-of-ten times.

The Long Beach Courthouse has a pleasant view of the Pacific Ocean and the Queen Mary, but in those days it was not a particularly safe place. Just walking from the parking structure to the court building everyday was always an adventure avoiding the ever-present and increasing number of homeless, pickpockets, drunks, beggars and panhandlers.

It was during this trial that I stopped carrying a wallet and any *extra change*. I was happy to have this trial over with and return to Santa Ana.

Ten

Classic Comparative Negligence

Pate v. Johnson (OCSC-NB Harbor/Verdict 11/1/1991)

Looking back now, *Pate v. Johnson* was the quintessential disputed automobile accident case. It arose out of a two-vehicle collision in the intersection of South Coast Drive and Fairview in Costa Mesa.

Plaintiff Jennifer Pate, a sixteen-year-old high school student, was operating her Toyota Celica eastbound on South Coast Drive west of the intersection with Fairview.

At the same time, defendant Robert Johnson, a self-employed drapery salesman, was driving his Chevrolet van westbound on South Coast Drive. Johnson had stopped in the left-turn lane behind another vehicle waiting for the red light. When the traffic signal changed, Johnson followed the vehicle ahead of him into the intersection; and waited for it to turn left.

Johnson was just beginning his left turn, when he observed the plaintiff's approaching vehicle. He immediately stopped to yield the right-of-way, but Pate continued on a straight course and collided with the front corner of Johnson's stopped van.

Because Pate was not seat-belted, upon impact, her face and chest impacted the steering wheel and her knees came in contact with the lower dashboard. As a result, she sustained neck and back sprains and strains, loss of a front tooth, knee laceration and contusion to her sternum.

Pate was represented at trial by Jeffrey W. Trombacco. He contended Pate didn't see Johnson's van until she was fifty feet from impact and the defendant violated plaintiff's right-of-way under the California Vehicle Code.

I argued to the jury that when Johnson stopped his vehicle—he *had* yielded the right-of-way to Pate—and thus he *was* in compliance with the vehicle code. Moreover, no other traffic prevented Pate from taking evasive action. She had an unobstructed view of Johnson for three-hundred feet and could have easily avoided the accident by stopping or steering her car around

Johnson's van. In addition, Pate was not wearing her seatbelt in violation of the vehicle code and that *caused* or contributed to her injuries.

To encourage settlement before starting trial, most personal injury actions are ordered by the judge to participate in a non-binding arbitration. The court randomly selects an arbitrator from a panel of attorneys who usually practice in that field. Sometimes you would get an arbitrator who was prejudiced against all defendants or just biased in favor of female plaintiffs.

This was one of those arbitrators, and despite the facts, and the obvious comparative negligence, she awarded Pate $94,000. Rarely did arbitrators explain the reasoning for their awards and this one was no exception. We disagreed with the arbitrator's decision and filed a request for Trial De Novo. The *De Novo* request nullified the arbitrator's award and the case was returned to the court's civil jury trial calendar.

The proceedings were held in the Orange County Superior Court-Newport Beach Harbor before the Honorable Richard Luesebrink. We had an interesting jury. One of the male jurors was a ventriloquist. He carried around a fake duck under his arm and entertained the other jurors when court was not in session.

Weeks before the trial began, we had offered the plaintiff $30,000 to settle, but it was rejected. Pate's counsel never lowered his settlement demand beneath the $94,000 arbitration award.

The trial lasted five days, but seemed much longer to me. In addition to Ms. Pate's testimony, her attorney called six expert witnesses, including a chiropractor, an orthopedist, a dentist, a vocational rehabilitation consultant, a forensic economist, and an accident reconstructionist.

To refute the opposing experts' opinions, we called our own orthopedic and dental consultants. I also called a bio-mechanical engineer who supported our affirmative defense that—*had* Ms. Pate been wearing her seatbelt—she would not have sustained injury.

I thought this case was straight forward; the deliberations would be short, and they would return quickly with a defense verdict. So, when their discussions dragged on for a day-and-a-half, I knew something was up—besides our juror's fake duck.

Pate's lawyer asked the jury to give her $140,000. Instead, they came back with an award for the plaintiff in the amount of $35,802. They also found young Ms. Pate to be fifty-percent at fault for the accident. Under the legal doctrine of comparative negligence, this meant Pate's *gross* verdict was cut in half for a *net* recovery of $17,901.

Since Pate did not obtain a net verdict in excess of the arbitration award ($94,000) or in excess of our pre-trial offer ($30,000), she was not entitled to recover her costs of suit or the cost of her expert witnesses. In fact, defendant Johnson was entitled to recover his costs from Pate.

Post-trial: Attorney Trombacco filed the usual post-trial motions asking the court to grant a new trial and award the plaintiff her costs and expert fees. I prepared and filed written opposition and Pate's motions were denied by the court. My client was satisfied with the trial results and I was off to my next trial.

It is worth noting here, that the cost of retaining and having six professional expert witnesses testify in court, far and away exceeded plaintiff's *net* verdict of $17,901. As a result, after paying her experts' fees, plus her litigation expenses, and her attorney—I doubt there was little, if any, money left over for Ms. Pate.

Whether this verdict would serve in the future as a gentle reminder to Mr. Trombacco to be more selective in the cases he took to trial is unknown.

Coincidently, almost twenty-five years later, I had another case with Mr. Trombacco. He seemed to have mellowed a bit since our last case, but he never once mentioned the *Pate* trial.

Eleven

Admitting Liability

Keily v. Rooten (OCSC-Santa Ana/Verdict 12/11/1991)

Most defense attorneys are reluctant to *admit liability* for many reasons; so, it was a rare occasion when we admitted the incident was our client's fault. In this case we had little choice.

Steven Rooten, a sixteen-year-old, from a well-to-do family, invited the plaintiff Mark Keily, also a sixteen-year-old high school student, to drive out to his parent's Lake Havasu vacation home for the weekend. They departed Orange County early morning. By 7:30 a.m. they were already between Needles, California and Parker, Arizona, when all occupants of the vehicle, including our driver, dozed off. Subsequently, the vehicle left the roadway and rolled over.

Miraculously, only Mr. Keily was injured, sustaining neck and back strains, lacerations to scalp and upper arm, as well as a concussion and heart contusion.

When the defense admits liability, the *only* issue left to litigate is the amount of *reasonable* and *necessary* damages the plaintiff is entitled to recover.

This makes for a much shorter trial and allows both sides to focus on the nature and extent of the plaintiff's injuries, medical treatment and bills. For example: Whether such injuries are temporary or permanent; whether they are physically disabling; and or whether the plaintiff can perform the same job duties or must be retrained.

To establish such evidence, the parties employ various expert witnesses to evaluate the damages and come into court and testify regarding their findings and conclusions.

Fortunately, this was not a serious injury case and the plaintiff's attorney, Warren C. "Chip" Dean, called only one expert witness—Mr. Keily's family physician Michael Grossman.

I disputed the nature and extent of the plaintiff's injuries and damages by getting him to admit he had no memory of the accident; had returned to all pre-accident activities; had graduated from high school on schedule;

enrolled in college; promoted as a grocery clerk; and engaged in all kinds of sports. His only residual complaints were healed scars on his upper bicep.

Attorney Dean asked the jury to award Mr. Keily damages in the range of $150,000-$200,000.

Before trial began, we had extended to the plaintiff a settlement offer of $35,000; but in my closing argument I suggested to the jury they award Keily $18,500. This stratagem came about during jury selection, when one of the prospective jurors expressed his strong personal belief that *"friends shouldn't sue friends."* I felt this statement could have an impact on the other jurors, who might feel the same way, but had not been as candid in sharing their opinion.

My gut feeling seemed to have paid off. Following a three day trial, the jurors deliberated for ninety minutes, before returning a verdict for Keily in the amount of $30,000.

The plaintiff did not recover an award greater than defendant's settlement offer, so he was not entitled to recover his costs of suit from defendant, and had to pay ours.

After the cost reduction, Keily's recovery was seven thousand dollars less than if he had accepted our pre-trial offer. This case was tried in Orange County Superior

Court-Santa Ana before the Honorable Donald Smallwood.

Post-trial: Months later, I received a nice note from the plaintiff Keily's attorney, Chip Dean, congratulating me on another jury trial I had recently won. Chip was a gentleman and a fine attorney.

Twelve

The Sandman Inn Motel

Jitendra Shelat v. Swo-Wei Chai (OCSC-Santa Ana/Verdict 6/30/1993)

Shelat v. Chai was an interesting trial on many levels. The named parties and witnesses sounded like *roll call* at the United Nations. The case involved one of the oldest motel properties in Anaheim, the *Sandman Inn Motel,* located down the street from Disneyland. The plaintiff Shelat alleged that defendant Chai misrepresented the motel's Disneyland marketing relationship at the time of sale resulting in lost bookings.

The plaintiff purchased the motel for $3.92 million and later contended it was worth $980,000 less *without* the Disneyland affiliation.

On March 3, 1988, Shelat, a fifty-year-old

businessman, submitted a written offer to Chai, a forty-year-old real estate investor, to purchase the *Sandman Inn Motel*. On March 12, 1988, after the expiration of the buyer's seven-day inspection period, Shelat met Chai for the first time. Although it was agreed escrow would close before April 27, 1988, Shelat had trouble getting financing, and escrow did not close as scheduled.

On May 4, 1988, Chai received a letter from the Walt Disney Travel Company stating the motel would be dropped from its recommended "economy hotel list" following an unsatisfactory inspection. Disney gave the motel the option of contacting the travel agency immediately and fixing the problems, but Chai failed to do so.

On June 17, 1988, escrow finally closed. Shelat took over operation of the motel, found the letter and contacted Disney Travel, but they said it was too late; Sandman's spot on the economy list had been filled by another motel.

Shelat had no prior motel management experience and frequently *comp'd*[6] rooms to friends and family. He also changed the motel's long held *"800"* telephone reservation number. Shelat eventually defaulted on his

---

[6] *Comp'd* in this context means "complimentary" or "at no cost."

note and Chai foreclosed and took back the motel.

Shelat then filed suit for fraud, negligent misrepresentation, breach of implied covenant of good faith and intentional misrepresentation, requesting damages of $980,000, plus potential punitive damages and attorney fees and costs.

This case was tried in the Orange County Superior Court-Santa Ana before the Hon. Ronald Bauer. Attorney Robert Balmuth represented Shelat.

During my case, I contended that there was no fraudulent concealment of the Disney Travel letter; because Chai thought the deal was dead due to Shelat's failure to obtain financing. Chai also claimed he showed the Disney letter to Shelat the day escrow closed and told him he could call and reinstate if he wanted.

On cross-examination, I succeeded in getting Mr. Shelat to admit that: 1. Chai did not make any untrue representations to him about the property; 2. He was unable to rebut our property appraiser's opinion that the Disney Travel Co. affiliation did not affect the appraised value of the motel; and 3. The continued affiliation with Disney was not a condition precedent of the purchase contract.

The court proceedings lasted eight days. The jury deliberated for six hours and found in favor of Mr. Chai on all counts.

Post-trial: The plaintiff filed motions for *Judgment Notwithstanding the Verdict, or in the alternative, Motion for New Trial.* We opposed those motions and they were denied by the court. Shelat did not appeal the verdict or the rulings on his post-trial motions and the case was finally over.

Unrelated to the Shelat trial, just days after the verdict, my firm, McKay Byrne & Graham, closed the Orange County office and transferred all the Santa Ana employees to its Los Angeles Mid-Wilshire headquarters.

I had a big decision to make. I loved working for the McKay firm and hated to leave, but since it would require me to commute daily from Riverside into L.A., I accepted a trial attorney position with the Inland Empire office of Farmers Insurance Company House Counsel located in San Bernardino.

Thirteen

Bait and Switch?

Rollins v. Richardson X-Ray Inc. (RSC-Central/Verdict 11/17/1995)

The plaintiff, Kathryn Rollins, a thirty-five-year-old, commercial bank loan officer, was driving a passenger van carrying her two minor children. It had been raining. When she was turning left at the intersection, the defendant's driver, Eugene Stewart, was approaching a stop sign at the same intersection. As he began slowing down, he locked up his brakes on the wet pavement, and slid into the side of Rollins' van.

At the scene, Rollins *denied* any injury and *refused* medical aid. Neither of her children were injured. The only damage was to the van's sliding passenger door.

At trial, we admitted liability for the accident, but adamantly disputed the nature and extent of injuries and damages Rollins was now claiming.

Should be an easy case to resolve—right?

It should have been, but it seems like personal injury attorneys are always thinking up new theories of liability and damages to drive up the value of their cases; and they are able to find a health care specialist to support the latest injury trend and order up costly treatment.

It so happened that in this case, the dysfunction or syndrome-of-the-month was—*fibromyalgia.* Medical opponents at the time called it a *waste basket* diagnosis, because its subjective complaints of wide-spread body pain and depression were confined almost exclusively to middle-aged females with history of depression and migraines.

There was a deep division in the medical community whether fibromyalgia was even a real diagnosis, since the symptoms are entirely *subjective* and there is no cure. In other words, if you hurt all over—and it can't be diagnosed as anything else—it must be fibromyalgia.

Before Rollins and her attorney came up with this new strategy, I had no reason to look at this case as anything other than a simple, garden variety, soft tissue injury. Rollins's settlement demand at arbitration was $27,500. We countered with an offer of $20,000. The arbitrator saw the same facts we did and awarded her

$15,000. Rollins rejected the arbitrator's decision.

Then, almost a year later, during the mandatory settlement conference, I learned for the first time that Rollins was now claiming a completely new injury and was being aggressively treated and billed by a new practitioner.

Rollins' attorney Kevin Croswell had decided not to share with us the *new* injury diagnosis (fibromyalgia), treatment, and medical bills. This backfired on him when the court granted our emergency motions to reopen discovery, obtain the new treatment records, have Rollins examined by our own doctor, and retake her deposition.

Over the years, I had encountered some pretty clever personal injury attorneys, but in my opinion, Croswell took the cake.

Between the arbitration and the trial, the plaintiff ran her medical bills up to $59,216. She was now claiming past-loss of earnings of $67,707 and future-loss of earnings of $992,147. For someone who *denied* any injury complaint and *refused* medical aid at the accident scene, Rollins was now claiming significant injuries and damages.

In addition, her settlement demand was now $250,000—almost *ten times* her arbitration demand just the year before. This was a completely different case from the one Rollins presented at arbitration.

We retained Edwin Krick, M.D., the head of rheumatology at Loma Linda University Medical Center, as our medical expert to dispel the fibromyalgia claim.

The case was tried in the Riverside Superior Court-Central before the Honorable Dennis McConaghy, a criminal department trial judge, on temporary assignment to this civil department. He was a fair judge and made some good evidentiary rulings.

The trial lasted eight days. The plaintiff barely received the minimum required nine votes needed for a civil verdict; if one more juror had held out, we would have had a hung jury.

Croswell had asked the jurors to award his client $1.25 million, but apparently, there was disagreement among them concerning the amount of damages. Instead of the $1.25 million requested, they awarded Rollins *only* $60,000 for her economic damages; and awarded her just $20,000 for all the non-economic damages she allegedly suffered as a result of the accident.

Post-trial: As the prevailing party, Rollins brought a motion asking the court to order the defendant to pay all $41,500 of her expert witness fees. Judge McConaghy, after several briefings, denied the plaintiff's motion on the grounds her initial offer to settle (for $27,500) was based on a totally different set of facts than the case she presented at trial.

In short, it appeared to me that her counsel's gamesmanship cost Rollins recovery of her expert fees of $41,500. Payment of those fees would now have to come out of the $80,000 verdict—from which she also had to pay her trial costs and medical bills—not to mention her attorney.

During the trial, a rumor circulated on the courthouse gossip line, that Rollins' lawyer had taken a loan out on his house to bankroll this trial. He was *swinging for the fences* which reminded me of an age-old legal maxim that says: "Pigs get fed. Hogs get slaughtered."

Online research also disclosed that Rollins filed an application for Social Security Administration Disability benefits in 1995. Her application was denied, then appealed, and denied again by the Ninth Circuit Court of Appeals, who concluded that Rollins was *not totally disabled* from fibromyalgia.

Finally, it is interesting to note that our jury never decided *if* Rollins had fibromyalgia.

After all the fuss, my initial case evaluation was correct—this *was* just a garden variety, low speed, minor impact, soft tissue injury automobile accident.

Fourteen

Melba's Toast[7]

Wiggins v. Waite (RSC-Central/ Verdict 1/14/1999)

Representing the plaintiff Melba Wiggins in this trial was one of the rising stars of the Beverly Hills plaintiff personal injury bar—Gary Dordick. He took over the handling of the case from Wiggins's first attorney after it was set for trial. That surprised me because this case did not seem to have a large enough dollar value to warrant such a high-profile attorney.

At the time of the incident, Wiggins, a sixty-two-year-old widow, was staying with friends in a rural area of Riverside County, where the properties are zoned for horses. While out for a walk one morning, she claimed

---

[7] *Melba Toast* is defined by the *Merriam-Webster Dictionary* as a "very thin crisp toast named after the Australian Dame Nellie Melba."

the defendant's four dogs (three Rottweilers and a Jack Russell Terrier) ran off the property and attacked her. She sustained multiple dog bites and scratches to her legs, abdomen and buttocks. In addition, she claimed the incident aggravated a pre-existing heart condition requiring her to be hospitalized on three occasions.

The judicially mandated and non-binding arbitration hearing was one I will never forget. It was conducted by Michael Pennell, a partner in the San Bernardino law firm of Klute & Pennell. At arbitration, Wiggins testified she had dog bites on her abdomen and buttocks and insisted the arbitrator see her battle scars. But, Mr. Pennell, with a straight face, told Wiggins, "If you were a 21-year-old run-way-model that might have some relevance here, but frankly madam, no one wants to look at your abdomen or buttocks." I could barely keep from laughing out loud. It still makes me chuckle when I think about it. Wiggins, indignant and flabbergasted, replied something like, "Well—I never."

The arbitration got even better. At the end of both parties' presentations, Mr. Pennell asked Wiggins's attorney how much he thought his client's case was worth and he replied, "$75,000." Then, Mr. Pennell inquired what I thought the case was worth assuming liability. I responded, "$15,000." Without missing a beat,

Mr. Pennell said, "Yes, that's what I think its worth."

Then he explained to the plaintiff attorney that, "Here in the Inland Empire, we evaluate cases differently than they do in L.A. For every mile a Beverly Hills attorney drives out here, it reduces the value of their case by $1000." Since Beverly Hills was sixty miles from San Bernardino, his case had declined in value from $75,000 to $15,000.

More often than not, defense attorneys get the proverbial *shaft* at these arbitrations; so, I could not stop smiling all the way back to the office. I never had so much fun at an arbitration hearing before or since.

After the arbitrator's award was issued, Ms. Wiggins's first attorney requested Trial De Novo and Mr. Dordick was brought in to try the case.

The action was set in Riverside County Superior Court-Central before one of the county's really great judges. Victor Miceli was the presiding civil law department judge and a legend at the downtown courthouse. He had just overseen the five-year renovation and restoration of the beautiful 1903 Riverside Historic Courthouse. I believe ours was the first jury trial conducted in Miceli's large and ornate Department One courtroom after it reopened.

For all the pre-trial hype, Mr. Dordick was good, but

like everyone else, he still put his pants on one leg at a time. At trial, he called only one expert witness, the plaintiff's internist. That required us to retain and call a cardiologist, Marvin Appel, M.D., to refute his opinions. We also used an excellent canine behavior consultant, Ron Berman.

The Waites contended their dogs never left their property, and therefore did not attack Wiggins. Moreover, she had walked by their property for six months without being assaulted. Also, there was another dog running loose in the neighborhood that day that could have bit her. The defendants observed Wiggins after the time of the alleged incident; she looked fine, and said nothing about being bitten by their dogs.

My canine expert testified that the defendants' dogs were non-territorial and non-aggressive; therefore, incapable of the type of attack described.

Finally, our medical expert, Dr. Appel, testified the incident did not aggravate Wiggins's pre-existing heart condition.

After a six day trial, Mr. Dordick told the jury to award Wiggins $150,000. The jury deliberated for one day and returned a verdict for the plaintiff in the amount of $23,256 ($8,256 for medical bills and $15,000 for her pain and suffering).

After the jurors were thanked and excused, we all went out into the hallway to talk to them about the trial. Then, Ms. Wiggins, the last person to exit the courtroom, in true *drama queen* style, swung open the large courtroom doors and burst out into the hallway shouting, "It's not over. It's not over. I'm going to appeal."

Post-trial: True to her word, Wiggins appealed the verdict *In Pro Per*[8]. But just a few months later, it was dismissed by the Court of Appeal.

On a personal note, two of my five children, Robert and Tina, attended a few days of this trial and got to see a couple of decent lawyers in action, some good courtroom drama, and great witness cross-examination. But apparently, it was not enough to convince them to follow their dad's footsteps into the practice of law.

---

[8] *In Pro Per* is a Latin phrase that essentially means Wiggins represented herself on the Appeal without a lawyer.

Fifteen

Against All Odds

Montano v. Garcia (LASC-Pomona/Verdict 7/21/2000)

If there ever was a *trial from hell*—it was *Montano v. Garcia*. The facts I had to work with are as follows: My client, the defendant Steven Garcia, was driving his vehicle while allegedly high on marijuana and alcohol, when he struck a sixty-two-year-old grandmother, the plaintiff Victoria Montano, pushing her two-year-old grandson, Mariano, in a stroller across the street in a marked crosswalk. The impact catapulted grandma and grandson down the road. Both of them suffered serious injuries. So, he's screwed, right?

It gets even worse. When we arrived at court on Monday to start trial, the clerk told us the judge would be late because she had broken a tooth over the weekend and was at the dentist. (The judge might be a little irritable?). We reconvened in the afternoon and went over some preliminary matters and then recessed until the next morning.

On Tuesday, the judge ruled on our pre-trial motion to exclude all evidence of alcohol and marijuana. She excluded mention of the alcohol, but allowed the weed. (If you are keeping score, I'm already six points down and we haven't kicked off yet).

During jury selection, I took a gamble and told the jury, "Look folks—I have a problem. My client hit a pedestrian in a crosswalk and we've all been taught that pedestrians have the right-of-way—right? "Yup," they said in unison. (Score is now: 9-0).

But then I asked them, "Is that assumption always true? What if the pedestrian was jaywalking? Or ignored the lights and sirens of an ambulance, fire or police vehicle? Or the pedestrian suddenly stepped into the path of an oncoming vehicle leaving the driver no time to react or distance to stop?" "Yes," some of the prospective jurors agreed, "there are circumstances where a pedestrian might have the right-of-way, but would be a fool to assert it."

Next, I told them, "I have another problem. The opposition is claiming my client was under the influence of marijuana. He admits to past use, but wasn't using on the day of the accident." (I'm thinking to myself, hey, I'm in Pomona, one of the more enlightened and liberal areas of East Los Angeles County—not Omaha, right?).

So, I'm expecting the jurors to say, "No big deal. I smoked a joint or two once myself." But, no. Not this time. The majority of the jurors said, "We would have a problem with that" or "That taints the defendant's character." (The score is now 12-0 plaintiff).

The trial began and the plaintiffs called six witnesses. On cross-examination, I got their traffic investigation officer to testify that "Garcia did not violate the Basic Speed Law." In other words, the defendant was "not speeding" at the time of the accident.

Under my cross-examination the plaintiffs' toxicology expert testified, "I can't say the marijuana caused the accident."

On Wednesday, Grandma Montano was called to the witness stand. She had suffered a serious injury (fractured leg), however, on cross-examination, Montano admitted the accident occurred at 10:30 p.m., on a dark and moonless night, the cross-walk was unlit, and she could see Mr. Garcia's headlights approaching a full quarter-mile to half-mile away before stepping off the curb.

But Montano's biggest admission was—although she was pushing her grandson in a stroller directly into the path of an oncoming vehicle—she *never* bothered to look in the direction of Garcia's car again to see if it was slowing down.

By Thursday, the plaintiffs finished up and I started the defense case by calling one of the police officers. Then I called my client to the stand. He turned out to be a much better witness than I expected. He was remorseful. Humble. Polite. And most importantly B-e-l-i-e-v-a-b-l-e.

The whole week I hadn't slept well, so by Friday, I was physically and mentally exhausted. I got up that morning and while taking a shower, the electricity went off in the house. The outage killed the phone, so I couldn't call my witnesses. When I arrived at court, I learned the elevators weren't working, and of course, we were on the top floor. I barely made it to our sixth-floor courtroom on time. This wasn't turning out to be a good start to my day.

There was still a big issue over the reasonableness of the medical bills and liens. The judge was losing patience fast and would not allow our medical expert to rebut the plaintiffs' evidence that the cost of a future knee replacement was $80,000. (The score is now 18-0 plaintiffs).

I called my last two witnesses. First, a forensic toxicologist, who testified the evidence *wasn't* sufficient for her to opine that Mr. Garcia was under the influence of marijuana at the time of the accident.

Second, our accident reconstruction expert, explained that it was *impossible* for Mr. Garcia to see Grandma Montano and bring his vehicle to a stop before this unlit cross-walk, on a moonless night, because Garcia's headlights would have only lit up the right lane he was traveling in—and Montano was crossing from the left lane.

During the lunch break, I went out to the parking lot, only to discover a flock of larger-than-average-size, dive-bombing birds, had been using my windshield for target practice. This was the final insult.

The case went to the jury that afternoon. While waiting for them to deliberate, the bailiff came over to me at the counsel table and whispered, "Son, you got a big problem, you have a retired police chief on the jury, and the negligence against your driver is a given." (The score is now: 24-0).

Just before 4:30 p.m., we were informed the jury had reached a verdict. I was prepared for the worst. Would it be an excess verdict? Would it be half-a-million dollars? Three-quarters of a million? I felt sick to my stomach.

After the formalities, I held my breath as the clerk read from the special verdict form these words: "Question No. 1: Was the Defendant Steven Garcia negligent? Answer to Question No. 1: No."

I was stunned. The bailiff couldn't believe it. I think the judge was stunned or maybe her tooth was still hurting? The plaintiff attorney was aghast. He had managed to lose what everyone, including me; thought was a slam dunk case. The plaintiffs were confused. The defendant was relieved.

After discussing the trial and the verdict with the jurors, and saying goodbye to my client, I got in my car and drove away thinking—this verdict really was *against all odds*.

For a defense attorney, it just doesn't get much better than this.

Sixteen

Pit Bull Terror

Jay/Ransom v. Bechard (RSC-Indio/Verdict 4/30/2002)

In April 2002, I left my position with Farmers Insurance Company house counsel and joined *Lewis Brisbois Bisgaard & Smith's* San Bernardino office. During the time I was with *Lewis Brisbois* (from 2002 to 2016), the firm grew from a six-office civil litigation firm to a thirty-six office national mega firm with more than a thousand attorneys. I was proud to be part of a large and well-known firm. My first year I tried three cases and made non–equity partner.

Jay v. Bechard was my first trial after the move. Hoping to make a good impression on my new employer, I wanted to win this case bad, but knew I couldn't. My clients were being sued after their dog, a pit bull pup, allegedly attacked and bit two teenaged girls. The California Dog-Bite Statute imposes statutory (automatic) liability on a dog owner and the best I could hope for was to minimize the damages.

My opposing counsel, Barry Regar, was an older, experienced, trial attorney based in Indian Wells, California, near Palm Springs. I had heard other defense lawyers describe Barry as a "legend in his own mind," primarily because he always demanded the insurance policy limit on every case, whether it was a broken fingernail or a broken neck. This dispute was no different and he left us no alternative but to defend the action.

The matter was scheduled for jury trial in the Riverside Superior Court–Indio Branch. Our assigned trial judge was the Honorable Lawrence Fry. I liked Judge Fry for a couple reasons. First, he seemed to be fair to both sides. Second, he had a great first name.

The case arose out of the following facts: My clients, Deborah Bechard and her adult son, Eric, were sued after Eric's eleven-month-old pit bull escaped from the backyard and allegedly attacked and bit two teenagers, Aiden Jay and Jennifer Ransom. There was no doubt they were bitten, but the circumstances of the attack were questionable.

Eric Bechard had moved to San Francisco to attend

culinary school and left his dog with his mother until he could find a place of his own. Mrs. Bechard's home was listed for sale at the time which gave realtors access to the house and rear yard via the lock box.

While speaking to Mrs. Bechard the day before the trial was to commence, she told me about a neighbor who had lived across the street at the time of the incident. She thought he might have seen the realtors leave the gate open, allowing the dog to escape. Mrs. Bechard did not have the ex-neighbor's new address or phone number, but somehow, I found it either in the phone book or by calling information.

In any event, literally the day before the trial was to commence, I called and met with the former neighbor at his new address. He provided the critical information we needed. In addition, he volunteered that he let his *preschool-age* children play with the Bechard's pit bull pup without hesitation. His testimony also diminished any assumption the dog had *vicious propensities*—prior bites or attacks.

At trial, I argued Deborah Bechard was neither the owner of the dog nor did she allow the dog to escape the yard. And, the most likely scenario was an unidentified real estate agent went into the backyard and left the gate ajar. In addition, she was not aware the dog had any vicious propensities. The former neighbor's testimony supported Mrs. Bechard's contentions. He also testified the dog must have been provoked for it to have attacked anyone.

The plaintiffs, ages twelve and sixteen, at the time of the alleged attack, were part of a group of teenagers hanging out in their front yard hitting golf balls. The girls didn't see the other kids strike the dog with the golf clubs, but admitted they weren't watching either.

It took weeks to obtain discovery orders from the court to compel the listing real estate broker to turn over the computerized front entry door keycard lock box information. The box would identify each realtor and the time of day they visited Bechard's property on the day of the incident. I was finally successful, but unfortunately the information recovered from the lock box was not helpful.

Our case was tried against a backdrop of dog bite hysteria brought on by a national news story out of San Francisco, where a woman was mauled to death by a large dog. By coincidence, there was also a rash of reported pit bull attacks across Riverside County.

In the S.F. case, the D.A.'s office criminally prosecuted the dog owner, but the trial was moved to L.A. after the court granted a change of venue. The S.F.

Assistant D.A. who tried the case was Kimberly Guilfoyle, who later became a well-known news commentator with the Fox News Channel.

Because of all the hysteria in the media, I fully expected the jurors to have an anti-dog prejudice, but to my surprise, most of them were either past or present dog owners. One prospective juror was a Palm Springs police officer, who disclosed he had to shoot a pit bull in the line-of-duty. Despite that revelation, after questioning him further in the judge's chambers, I kept him on the jury.

At trial, Mr. Regar asked the jury to award Aiden Jay $211,988 (the equivalent of ten-dollars-a-day for fifty years plus medical bills); and to award Jennifer Ransom $36,784 (the equivalent of ten-dollars-a-day for ten years plus medical bills). The dollar amounts requested by Mr. Regar surprised me, since his initial settlement demands had always been the half million-dollar policy limit for each plaintiff. In short, I believe had he just been reasonable at the outset of the case, the trial could have been avoided.

In my closing address to the jury, I argued the facts that Mrs. Bechard could not be held liable, because she was not the dog owner, and there was no evidence she allowed the dog to escape.

Next, I contended that although Eric Bechard was the undisputed dog owner, there was no evidence he allowed the dog to escape. In the alternative, I argued that if they found Eric liable, then Ms. Jay's general damage case was worth $25,000 and Ms. Ransom's was worth $5000.

After seven days of trial, the jury deliberated for one day and awarded the plaintiffs—*exactly* the amount of general damages I suggested in my closing argument.

Moreover, the jurors found Mrs. Bechard had no liability. In addition, Aiden's mother, Billie Jay, had asserted a claim for negligent infliction of emotional distress, but the court granted our non-suit motion, since Billie did not witness the dog bite Aiden.

At the beginning of the trial, Mr. Regar tried to disqualify my defense canine behavior expert, but the court denied his motion.

Post-trial: Since we successfully defended Mrs. Bechard, the plaintiffs were not entitled to recover their trial costs or experts fees.

To his credit, Mr. Regar did not appeal the verdicts, and the case came to an end.

I was blessed again to locate a witness, who was not only favorable, but willing to testify at the last minute. I give all the credit to the Bechards, who were not only nice people—but good neighbors as well. It helps when the jurors like your clients.

In view of the disadvantages I faced coming into this trial, namely the canine hysteria prevalent in the media and the dog-bite statute, I was more than pleased with the outcome.

My confidence in the integrity of the jury system continued to expand.

Seventeen

The Snow Bird

Peters v. Lusk (RSC-Indio/Verdict 2/26/2004)

This trial was another *duel in the Indio desert*. The plaintiff, Frank Peters, was a retired millionaire from Colorado, who kept a vacation home in the Palm Springs area. No one would have known he was from out-of-state, but for the Colorado license plates on his shiny new BMW.

One morning after having breakfast at a popular local diner, Peters backed his car out of his parking space and into Leroy Lusk's not so new, but still classic, red Cadillac. Peters contended Lusk backed into him—but he had no eyewitnesses to support his claim.

Peters himself was a non-practicing lawyer. He hired not one, but two, aggressive personal injury attorneys to sue Mr. Lusk, and as they say, we were *off to the races.* Peters acted like he was prepared to spend whatever amount it took to win.

From talking to the desert locals, I knew they didn't particularly care for the *snow birds* who descended on their fair city during the winter months. So, I had a color photograph of the dent on the rear of Mr. Peters's BMW blown-up that prominently displayed his Colorado license plate.

Leroy Lusk was an older gentleman who suffered from a condition similar to Tourette's syndrome. Several times during the trial, while the plaintiff or his witnesses were testifying, Mr. Lusk would suddenly blurt out loud—"that's bullshi*" or "that's a God d*** lie." I had to remind him constantly not to say anything, but I don't think he even knew he was doing it.

Peters was represented by an ex-Marine, Don C. Burns, and a second lawyer, Glen Robinson. During trial, they pulled some monkey business I had not seen before. For example: in an apparent attempt to engender sympathy for their alleged injured client, they arranged for handicapped people to stroll in-and-out of the courtroom during various phases of the trial. These were people on crutches or wearing an arm sling or cervical collar. While such gimmicks in and of themselves do not violate any court or ethical rule, in my opinion, they just aren't necessary if you have a strong case.

Next, they had one of their female legal assistants surreptitiously chat up my male expert witness on the benches in the hallway outside the court room, while he patiently waited his turn to testify. Now this was pushing the envelope. The Rules of Professional Conduct provide that a party is not to have contact with the other side or his witnesses except through opposing counsel.

Last, but not least, after the trial was over, and the jurors were free to talk to the parties and attorneys, one of the male jurors came up to me as I was leaving the courthouse. He informed me Mr. Burns had approached him at the gym that morning before court and engaged him in conversation. In my opinion, this was clearly a violation of the Rules of Professional Conduct—since attorneys are prohibited from any ex-parte contact with a juror until after the trial is over.

The plaintiff attorneys started off their case-in-chief by calling Mr. Lusk. I'm sure they thought the old man would wilt under the blistering heat of their cross-examination. But, despite counsel's repeated questioning, Lusk remained adamant that he was all-the-way-out of his parking space, *before* Peters backed into him.

The plaintiff then called his treating physician, Dr.

Wilgarde, who was unable to provide testimony regarding *causation* or lay a proper evidentiary foundation for admissibility of the substantial past-medical bills.

Next, Mr. Peters took the witness stand and told his version of the accident and his four-year journey to neck surgery. When it was my turn, I had some fun with him on cross-examination. First, I got Mr. Peters to admit there were no eyewitnesses to the incident—so it was just his word against Mr. Lusk's. Second, I pointed out that his own medical records documented he had degenerative disc disease long before the cars bumped in the parking lot. Third, I got him to concede that before the accident he made a complaint of neck pain to his doctor after hitting a hundred golf balls at the driving range. Fourth, I pointed out that his neck surgeon at UCLA declined to come testify that this very low speed, minor impact, in a parking lot, caused an injury necessitating neck surgery—four years later.

Mrs. Peters took the stand next and tried to explain away the inconsistencies in her husband's testimony, but admitted she didn't see the incident.

After my cross-examination, Peters's attorneys announced they were resting their case. I immediately moved for non-suit, but the court denied on the grounds that causation can be established even by conjecture. However, our additional motion to exclude the *past-*medical bills for lack of proper foundation, *was* granted.

The following day, I began the defense case by calling our orthopedic medical examiner, Dr. Gettleman, who testified the minor bump-on-the- trunk did not cause the injury that resulted in neck surgery four years post-accident.

The plaintiff's cross-examination was particularly vicious. Instead of trying to discredit the doctor's opinions or credentials, they attacked him personally. They questioned him about one of their former clients whose case didn't pan out for them after receiving a poor evaluation by Dr. Gettleman. The opposing attorney's cross-examination was long and tedious, but our medical expert held his ground well.

Next, I called our accident reconstruction and bio-mechanic expert, Rob Harrison. The plaintiff's lawyer challenged his credentials in bio-mechanics and took him on a 402 hearing outside the presence of the jury. But their challenge backfired when the court ruled in our favor—finding Mr. Harrison was well qualified.

My expert went on to demonstrate to the jury how the impact between the two vehicles would have produced *only* about one "G" of force. He explained how our bodies experience more force than that in routine daily activities.

He also testified Mr. Lusk's version of the incident was the only one consistent with and supported by the physical evidence. Although the plaintiff's cross-examination of this expert witness was also tedious and aggressive, nevertheless, even two plaintiff attorneys were no match for an experienced trial expert like Mr. Harrison.

Finally, I called Mr. Lusk's daughter to the witness stand. She had been at the restaurant with her father before the incident, and left, but returned to the scene after her father called her. Upon arrival, she observed Mr. Lusk speaking to Mr. Peters, but never saw Mrs. Peters. I then announced that Mr. Lusk was resting his case.

But the trial wasn't over yet. The plaintiff called rebuttal witnesses. Our opposition to the first rebuttal witness, Jetha Hoffman, was successful. She was the disgruntled former personal injury client of opposing counsel, who had been examined by Dr. Gettleman.

Next, the court over my objection, allowed counsel to call Dr. Probst, who had examined Mr. Peters once—more than four years prior. The plaintiff attorneys were hoping this doctor could do what Doctor Wilgarde couldn't—establish causation and lay a foundation for the past medical bills. But the best he could do was speculate if Mr. Peters had his neck turned and had his arm extended when the bump occurred, it could possibly have increased the risk of injury to his neck.

My cross-examination was short and straight forward. I was about to sit down, when a thought suddenly popped into my mind to ask Dr. Probst two questions. First question—"Sir, *when* were you retained by Mr. Peters to testify in this case?"

Second question—"How *much* are you being paid by Mr. Peters for your testimony today?" The doctor replied he was just contacted—"late yesterday afternoon" and Mr. Peters was paying him—"*Ten Thousand Dollars.*"

You could hear the jurors' collective gasp. The response—"*Ten Thousand Dollars*"—hung heavy in the afternoon air; and the day ended for us on a high note thanks to some great cross-examination.

The next day, both sides gave their closing arguments. The attorneys for Mr. Peters suggested the jury should award him $80,000 in *future*-medical bills plus $200,000 for his pain and suffering.

When it was my turn, I argued to the jury Peters was the sole *cause* of the accident and any injuries and damages he incurred. Therefore, he should get nothing.

The jury began their deliberations about 3:00 p.m. Ten minutes later, they had a question about exhibits. One hour later, they returned with a verdict—for the defendant Mr. Lusk.

Post-trial: A few weeks after the judgment was entered for the defendant, Peters filed a motion asking the court to grant him a new trial on the grounds he thought he should have won. The court followed my opposing points and authorities and swiftly denied his motion. Peters, undeterred, then filed a notice of appeal, but within thirty days the appeal was abandoned, and the case was finally over.

Since Mr. Lusk was the prevailing party, we were entitled to recover not only our costs of suit, but also our expert fees. We sent our cost bill to opposing counsel and a short time later received back a personal check from Mr. Peters for the full amount.

This trial taught me to always listen to that little voice in my head, follow my instincts, and push myself to do the best for the client, despite being outnumbered by the opposition three-to-one.

Eighteen

She Missed the Bus

Ochoa v. Omnitrans, et. al. (SBSC-R.C./Verdict 11/22/2006)

This trial featured a rematch with Gary Dordick—the plaintiff attorney from the *Melba Wiggins* case. The lawsuit was tried in front of a retired Court of Appeals Justice, the Honorable Kenneth William Andreen, sitting by temporary assignment, due to a shortage of trial judges in San Bernardino County. Judge Andreen was old, grumpy, and hard of hearing.

At the time of the incident, plaintiff, Yolanda Ochoa, a married, fifty-one-year-old, temp agency employee, was a passenger on the defendant Omnitrans' public transit authority bus. The driver, James Montgomery, was approaching the intersection of Chino and Magnolia Avenues in the City of Chino, when a Chevy Caprice, driven by the co-defendant, Helena Abilez, suddenly pulled out from a stop sign and into the path of the oncoming bus. The Chevy was *T-boned.* The resulting impact knocked Ochoa off her bus seat causing her to strike her collar bone against a stanchion.

Ochoa was transported by ambulance from the scene to the hospital and treated for a broken collarbone. She was released from the E.R. the same day. Unfortunately, due to non-union of the fractured collarbone, Ochoa later underwent corrective surgery. At trial, she claimed continuing residual physical complaints.

Miraculously, despite her vehicle being hit by a bus, and not wearing her seat belt, the other driver Ms. Abilez was shaken, but unharmed by the impact. Abilez, a young substitute teacher, was en route to a new school assignment that morning.

She was driving her father's vehicle and the dark-tinted side windows made it difficult to see out. Abilez admitted she came to a full stop at the intersection, checked for oncoming traffic, but *missed* the oncoming bus—before pulling out into the intersection. She also admitted being temporarily blinded by the morning sun.

Her father's automobile insurance carrier settled with Ochoa, and as a result, Abilez was not a party to the trial.

Despite the settlement between Ochoa and Abilez—and her admission of fault—the plaintiff pursued Omnitrans as the *deep pocket*[9] defendant.

Moreover, even though our bus had the green light and the right-of-way, Ochoa contended the bus driver was traveling too fast for conditions, and could have stopped the bus before striking the Abilez vehicle. I adamantly disputed these contentions and denied any negligence on the part of our driver.

Both sides retained accident reconstruction experts to support their respective positions at trial. The plaintiff's expert contended this intersection fell within a school speed zone. I showed the jury it didn't. Ochoa's expert also contended if the bus driver had started braking sooner, then the Abilez vehicle would have crossed through the intersection without collision.

My professional engineer opined that the bus driver was traveling within the posted speed limit, had the right-of-way, and did not have enough time to *perceive and react* to avoid the accident. Thus, the bus driver reacted properly under the circumstances.

After a tumultuous back-and-forth five-day trial, Mr.

---

[9] A *deep pocket* is a commonly used slang term that refers to a business or governmental entity that has sufficient financial wealth or resources to satisfy a large verdict.

Dordick asked the jury to award the plaintiff $3.8 million. That amount included damages for past-and-future pain and suffering, $34,859 for past-loss of earnings, $50,000 for past-medical costs, and $1 million for *future* medical costs which included gastrointestinal, psychiatric, and physical therapy treatment, as well as, the installation of a personal exercise gym in Ochoa's house.

The jury was out just two hours before coming back with a verdict for the defense. This was a nice way to begin the Thanksgiving holiday.

Post-trial: Our bus driver left the company sometime after the accident and by the time the case came to trial he had disappeared. Contact with people living at his last known address told us Mr. Montgomery had passed away. This was a disadvantage we overcame by explaining his absence during jury selection and asking each juror if that would be a problem for them.

Nineteen

The Stalker

Adams v. Fernandez (SBSC-R.C./Verdict 11/16/2007)

Despite the serious nature of this matter, I enjoyed working this case up for trial for several reasons. There were definitely some interesting twists and turns. This case had what attorneys call *sex appeal*—and how. It is the story of a hero and a villain. It is a tale of passion and unrequited love.

The plaintiff Paul Adams and the defendant Mike Fernandez were both attracted to the same woman. I'll call her *Summer* (not her real name). The problem is, Summer wasn't interested in Adams—and as the lyrics to the popular hit song *The Power of Love* says—"Love can make one-man weep and another man sing."

Adams wasn't singing. He was way out of his league

and he let Summer's rejection get to him. He was clearly fixated and began stalking her. She got a restraining order and he would violate it. She got another. He violated it and was arrested.

Summer moved on and began a relationship with my client. It all came to a head when Fernandez, Summer and Adams came face-to-face at the wedding of a mutual friend held at the bride's home.

Approximately six weeks before the confrontation, Adams was arrested twice for stalking Summer and had been ordered to stay away. When she moved, he would find her. When she changed her phone number, he would find that too. She had no peace before and now he was angry for being arrested and threatening her. Summer had good reason to be afraid.

The day of the wedding, Adams told another guest he was going to "get even" with Summer for having him arrested by running her car off the road.

Summer had only agreed to be the bride's maid-of-honor on the condition Adams was not invited. Unbeknownst to Summer and the bride, the groom had invited Adams. Upon their arrival at the wedding, Mike and Summer were surprised to see Adams. He was already intoxicated and in a rage came right up to them making crude remarks and threats before the wedding started.

Concerned about Adams's aggressiveness, Mike and Summer decided to skip the reception and leave immediately after the wedding ceremony. As they were departing, Adams walked out to his pickup truck and removed two long-neck bottles of beer from an ice chest. He approached the couple in a threatening manner, shouting epitaphs, while raising the beer bottles into a striking position. But before Adams could harm him or Summer—Fernandez with a single blow—knocked Adams down, breaking his nose and inflicting a gash on his cheek. Adams and Fernandez were both arrested at the scene for assault and battery, but the D.A. later dismissed the charges on the grounds of *mutual combat*.

Adams wasted no time filing a civil suit against Fernandez for assault and battery, false arrest, emotional distress and punitive damages. In our answer to Adams's complaint, we asserted the civil law affirmative defenses of *self-defense* and *defense of others*.

During pre-trial discovery, the attorney for Adams subpoenaed Summer for deposition. Normally the plaintiff is entitled to be present when a witness is questioned by his attorney. But after I received a phone call from Summer advising me she was scared to death to be in the same room with Adams, I filed a motion for a *protective order.* We asked the judge to exclude Adams from Summer's deposition under the circumstances, citing the previous harassment and violation of the restraining orders. The judge agreed that Adams should be excluded, but he could watch the deposition at another location via closed circuit video.

As I suspected all along, setting Summer's deposition was just a *pre-text* by Adams to get close enough to intimidate her. As a result of the court's exclusion ruling, his ruse failed, and Summer's deposition never went forward.

Adams's attorney also set up the depositions of other wedding guests. One of those guests was a recently retired L.A.P.D. detective, whom I will call *Felix* (not his real name). I arrived early for Felix's deposition and bumped into him waiting outside the plaintiff attorney's office. I had not been able to locate or take Felix's statement since the police department doesn't give out officer information without a court order. So, I didn't know what he was going to say about the incident.

Fortunately, before his deposition started, Felix told me that he was one of the groomsmen at the wedding and observed Adams's conduct leading up to the incident. In fact, Felix was standing next to Fernandez and Summer when Adams approached them with the beer bottles raised in a threatening and aggressive manner.

In Felix's opinion, Fernandez and Summer would have been in *reasonable fear* of serious bodily harm, justifying Fernandez's action to defend himself and Summer. How lucky can we be? Felix also just happened to be a police expert in *stalking* cases, and in his opinion, Adams fit the classic stalker profile.

If we were making a movie, we could not have ordered a better witness from *Central Casting*. Felix's testimony came across extremely credible at trial. If the jurors hadn't already made up their minds about Adams, this was the so called *icing on the cake*.

Unfazed, Adams's attorney asked the jury to award his client half-a-million dollars, plus his medical bills, and the cost of a lost job contract. After eight days of trial, the jurors deliberated for two days before returning a *unanimous* 12-0 verdict in favor of the defendant.

Post-trial: As the prevailing party we sent Adams the bill for our trial costs.

Once again, this case reinforced the lesson that you can never anticipate everything that might happen in pre-trial discovery or during trial. In addition, I was learning to read *body language* and I could tell the jurors were turned off by Adams's conduct—not to mention him wasting their valuable time with a frivolous lawsuit. The jury rightly concluded that Mr. Adams was the *villain* and Mr. Fernandez was the *hero* of this story.

This case was tried in the San Bernardino Superior Court-Rancho Cucamonga before the Hon. Martin Hildreth. I think it noteworthy to mention that the day before Summer came into court to testify for the defense, Judge Hildreth on his own motion (sua sponte) and outside the presence of the jury, sternly admonished and ordered Mr. Adams not to approach, speak to, stare at, or in any other way try to intimidate her.

Twenty

Stacking the Deck

Glover v. Villa Valencia Redlands HOA (SBSC/Verdict 4/16/2013)

Erma Glover was a very nice, white haired, seventy-four-year-old widow, who lived alone in my client's newly constructed gated townhome community. She looked like everyone's grandma, and that alone, made her an appealing and sympathetic witness. Glover claimed while taking her trash out one night, she fell down inside the dumpster enclosure. She suffered a comminuted multiple-fracture of her left humerus (upper arm) requiring open reduction and internal fixation with a metal plate and screws. She claimed residual on-going pain and weakness at the fracture site. Her bills for medical treatment totaled more than $104,000.

Glover's attorneys contended the design of the trash

enclosure was unreasonably dangerous, the lighting was inferior, and the Homeowners Association (HOA) should have installed tactile mats and handrails, despite the fact there had been no prior falls or complaints.

Initially, I thought we would get out of the case early, because the HOA neither designed nor built the townhouse community. The developer created the HOA to maintain the common areas, and Glover's complaint made no claim regarding a failure to maintain the dumpster enclosure.

Premises Liability law provides that before a property owner (including a HOA) can be held liable for injury or damage, they must have prior *actual* or *constructive* notice of a problem with the alleged common area.

In addition, they must have a reasonable time after discovery to remedy the condition. Here, the HOA had received no prior complaint of any problem with the dumpster enclosure. Moreover, the alleged condition would have been *open and obvious* to the plaintiff.

Our initial defense strategy included shifting liability to the developer and builder. Unfortunately, both had filed bankruptcy before trial. Subsequently, we offered Glover $25,000 to buy our peace and get the HOA out of the case, but Glovers' attorneys rejected our offer and countered with an unrealistic settlement demand of $550,000. That left us no option than to defend the case.

In court, Glover was represented by two experienced attorneys and a good paralegal. Their legal team spared no expense on a high-tech trial presentation.

Three-against-one are odds I had faced before, but in my opinion, from the outset, the trial judge did everything she could to help the plaintiff. For example, she denied all of our pre-trial motions, including one to exclude a videotape taken hours after the incident that neither showed the interior of the trash enclosure nor the lighting condition at the time of the incident.

Next, the court denied our request to introduce the *911 call*—produced in discovery by the plaintiff. Then, she overruled all of our objections to the plaintiff's evidence. The court denied all of our special jury instructions, as well as, our objections to the plaintiff's instructions.

On the other hand, the judge sustained every objection made by the plaintiff's counsel. She allowed the medical bills into evidence even when the custodian of those records could not say the charges were reasonable or necessary. She allowed opposing counsel to introduce non-relevant evidence of subsequent repairs to the premises.

But the *coup de grace*[10] occurred when my client caught the judge signaling to the plaintiff attorney when to object during my cross-examination of his witnesses, and then of course, sustaining his objections.

After all this piling on, I started to get that hopeless sinking feeling in my gut. I couldn't see now how we could possibly win. At least if we lost, there would be plenty of grounds for appeal. The plaintiff seemed to have everything going her way, the sympathy, the grandma thing, and even the judge.

A good lesson learned early is never let the opposing attorney, the judge, and especially the jury, see you lose confidence in your case. Stay positive, keep smiling, and have faith that you can win no matter what.

The one thing in this case the judge couldn't deny— was the jury verdict. After nine frustrating days of trial for the defense and waiting another day-and-a-half of deliberations, the jurors came to an 11-1 decision for the defendant HOA.

Post-trial: After the jury was thanked and dismissed, it didn't surprise me when the judge invited counsel for the plaintiff to speak privately with her in chambers and

---

[10] *Coup de grace* is defined by the *American Free Dictionary* as: 1. A deathblow delivered to end the misery. 2. A finishing stroke or decisive event.

excluded me.

The verdict was not appealed, probably because the plaintiff and her attorneys had been given every possible advantage at trial and had no grounds on which to file an appeal.

We won, but I never forgot the lesson this case taught me—be prepared for anything—including the trial judge stacking-the-deck against you.

Twenty-one

I Can Get You $2.5 Million

Jensen v. Omnitrans, et. al. (SBSC/Verdict 11/08/2013)

Around three o'clock on a February afternoon, Ronald Jensen, a seventy-one-year-old retired man, was driving his 2002 Saturn. His forty-one-year-old, unemployed son, Steven Jensen, was in the front passenger seat.

They were stopped behind another vehicle for a red traffic light at the intersection of Fifth Street and Arrowhead Avenue in downtown San Bernardino (just two blocks from the courthouse). Stopped directly behind the Jensens was a First Transit Inc. medical transport van. Cecilia Rodriguez was the driver and an Omnitrans employee.

The Jensens alleged when the traffic light turned

green, they were rear-ended by the transport van. Omnitrans and Rodriguez contended when the traffic light turned green, the Jensen vehicle moved forward a few feet, then stopped suddenly for no apparent reason. Our driver could not avoid colliding with the Saturn. The front camera on the medical transport van recorded the collision sequence.

After this minor impact the Jensens fled the scene. Ronald returned about fifteen minutes later, noticeably without Steven. This scenario raised several questions. Steven Jensen was recently released from prison and may not have had a valid driver's license. This led us to believe Steven was the driver and Ronald was the passenger. Steven probably didn't want to get caught driving without a license and violate his parole, so he sped off and drove out of sight. Then they stopped, changed drivers, and Steven took a walk to buy tacos.

Neither of the Jensens claimed *any* injury at the scene. In fact, they *refused* medical aid.

In these automobile personal injury cases the typical post-accident scenario goes something like this: The *uninjured* Jensens go home and happen to mention to a friend, relative, or neighbor that they were just hit by a *bus*. The friend, relative, or neighbor then tells the Jensens, "Dude, you need to call my L.A. lawyer. He can get you $2.5 million." "But we aren't injured," say the Jensens. "No matter" says the friend, relative, or neighbor, "I wasn't either bro—but my lawyer still got me the money." "Hum," reply the retired and unemployed Jensens in unison who then ask, "What's your lawyer's number?"

In this case, the Jensens *did* get a L.A. lawyer, who sent them to his doctors in Los Angeles. As a result, overnight, Ronald Jensen went from having no complaint of injury and refusing medical aid at the scene—to now being a candidate for shoulder surgery to repair a torn labral tear. Ronald then underwent microsurgery to decompress the injury at a L.A hospital, despite the fact he had access to unlimited medical care at no cost at the veteran's hospital in Loma Linda just a few miles from his house. Ronald's medical bills from the L.A. doctors and hospital totaled an exorbitant $98,000.

Steven Jensen also had no injury complaint at the scene and sought no medical care before his attorney referred him to a chiropractor. There, he was diagnosed with lumbar (lower back) disc bulges at L3-4, L4-5 and L5-S1 vertebra levels. Steven then underwent decompression and fusion surgery at the same L.A. hospital as Ronald, even though he had state and federal health care benefits available to him at no cost. His medical bills totaled more than $400,000.

The Jensens' L.A. lawyer filed suit against the transit authority and Rodriguez demanding $1 million for Ronald Jensen and $4 million for Steven Jensen. These unreasonable and inflated settlement demands left the defendants no alternative than to fight back.

At trial, I argued to the jury that Ronald's right shoulder injury was not caused by the accident, but rather was age-related and from overuse on the job. In other words, this was a pre-existing condition unrelated to the automobile accident.

Likewise, I contended Steven's lower back complaints were due to pre-existing problems and the back surgery was not only unrelated—but unnecessary.

I also contended the medical care was all attorney directed, involving a network of lawyers, doctors and hospitals, including a medical factoring company. Finally, I argued the medical charges were excessive and intentionally overbilled to artificially drive up the value of the plaintiffs' cases.

The Jensens had two very good trial attorneys who put on a high-tech audio/visual power-point presentation for the jury. Not to be outdone, the defense called top-notch medical, accident reconstruction and bio-mechanical experts to refute the plaintiffs' contentions. It was an expensive case for both sides.

After eight days of trial and two days of deliberations, the jury returned a verdict finding the Omnitrans driver *was* negligent for rear-ending the Jensens—but also found the minor impact between the van and the Saturn *did not* cause the extent of injuries the plaintiffs were claiming.

This was a big win. The transit authority's refusal to buckle under immense pressure to settle, forced the plaintiffs to go to trial and prove their case in front of a jury of their peers. That decision and our well-crafted defense saved the bus company $5 million dollars.

This trial reinforced my faith in the jury system and confirmed to me that more often than not—the *twelve strangers in the box* get it right.

Twenty-two

Dream House

Garcia v. JR Real Estate Partners, Inc. (SBSC/Verdict 1/23/2015)

When I took this case, little did I know that it would be my last jury trial. It was certainly challenging and required me to draw upon my experience from fifty-two previous jury trials. I also enjoyed the opportunity during this trial to mentor a smart young defense attorney, Randy Lopez, who was trying his first case. Looking back now, it was like passing the baton to the next generation.

In this lawsuit, I represented the defendants, JR Real Estate Partners, Inc. and Towne Center Property Management Co. (TCPM). They owned and managed the two-hundred-unit apartment complex where the plaintiff Garcia resided. Randy represented a separate defendant,

All Valley Washer Service, Inc., (AVWS) who contracted with my clients to place coin-operated washers and dryers in the apartment complex laundry rooms. AVWS would regularly inspect and maintain the machines. If repairs were needed, the apartment manager would contact them.

One evening, Alondra Garcia, took a basket of dripping wet clothes down stairs to the laundry room. After starting the dryer, she returned to her apartment. She came back twice to feed the dryer more coins. The third time she came back, she put the dry clothes in her laundry basket, turned towards the door, took a few steps and fell. Garcia assumed she slipped on water coming from a leaky washing machine. Her attorneys filed suit alleging negligent maintenance against my clients and Randy's.

Garcia claimed she sustained closed head, shoulder, neck, back and knee injuries as a result of her fall. She also claimed she broke her nose, requiring septoplasty.

This might sound like a clear-cut slip and fall negligence lawsuit, but this case had more twists and turns than a box of pretzels. From the beginning we were dealing with an opposing counsel who thought he knew everything and told us so. When I pointed out that he had erroneously sued the wrong business entities, he refused to admit it or amend his complaint; because in my opinion for him to do so would have caused irreparable damage to his extensive ego.

As a result, the case dragged on for the next twelve months until he was forced to realize we were right.

Because good defense lawyers are always trying to get their client out of the lawsuit by shifting fault to someone else—I filed a cross-complaint for indemnity against Randy's client. AVWS had contracted with my clients, but after our discovery revealed they had no contractual duty to indemnify us, I ended up dismissing them. Nevertheless, AVWS remained a defendant in the case under Garcia's complaint.

There arose several unique civil procedure pleading issues during this case, but I fear they would probably be of interest only to the lawyers and bore everyone else. In short, the plaintiff's lawsuit went to trial against only my client, TCPM and Randy's client, AVWS.

The *pre-trial* work up of a civil case by the defense consists basically of two phases: The first phase begins with the filing of an Answer to the Complaint on behalf of the proper and correctly named defendant business entities and/or individuals. After the Answer is filed at the courthouse, formal discovery begins.

During this second phase, both sides are allowed to

request information from each other. This is done by exchanging formal written questions known as Interrogatories, written Requests for Documents and Things, Requests for Physical Examinations and Notice of taking Depositions.

Through the discovery process, we were able to ascertain the true nature and extent of Ms. Garcia's injuries and damages, as well as, pin her down on the mechanics and causation of her alleged slip and fall. Discovery can be the longest phase of civil litigation, because if the opposing attorneys or their clients are not forthcoming with the requested information, then the opposing party is forced to bring time-consuming motions asking the court to order the offending party to comply.

While written discovery is underway, experts are consulted to review the physical evidence and render certain medical and liability opinions for trial. Here, the plaintiff's attorney retained medical and accident reconstruction consultants. This required the defense to retain reciprocal opposing experts to refute their opinions.

The first day of a civil trial is usually taken up with the judge exploring last-minute settlement discussions. This is the so-called *settlement on the courthouse steps.*

Our case was no different. The judge inquired, "What is the plaintiff's settlement demand?" Garcia's attorney replied, "$250,000." Then the judge asked the defense, "Do you have any interest in pursuing that offer?"

In California, we have *Code of Civil Procedure Section 998*—which encourages litigants to settle *before* trial by attaching enticements and penalties.

For example: If the plaintiff offers to compromise his or her case before trial for $250,000, and the defense turns the offer down, and the plaintiff then proceeds to trial and recovers *more than* $250,000, the defendant reaps the penalty and must pay all of the plaintiff's expert witness fees. And vice versa; if the plaintiff does not recover more than the defendant's offer, then the plaintiff must pay her own expert witness fees, as well as, the defendant's.

In this case, neither TCPM nor AVWS were interested in Plaintiff's settlement demand. We both accepted the inherent risks under C.C.P. 998 should Garcia be awarded more than our respective $20,000 pre-trial offers.

After the judge's informal settlement conference, but before jury selection began, the plaintiff's attorney told us Garcia would settle for $200,000, and wanted "six figures" from each defendant. This latest settlement demand was also declined by both defendants. Nevertheless, even after the trial began, Randy's client, AVWS, continued to negotiate with opposing counsel, first offering $25,000, then $50,000, and finally $75,000. Garcia's attorneys rejected those offers and chose to spin the proverbial litigation *roulette wheel*.

Besides last-minute settlement discussions, the first day of trial also includes the judge ruling on the parties' Motions in Limine (MIL). These motions seek to limit or preclude the other side's presentation of evidence. In this matter, the court denied all of the plaintiff's MIL and granted all but two of ours.

In addition, the court chose to read to the jury the *Statement of the Case* I prepared, rejecting the plaintiff's as *too* argumentative.

At the last minute, the plaintiff's attorney tried to amend their witness list to add four more witnesses, but the court allowed him to add only one—Garcia's husband. I felt good about the judge's rulings on these pre-trial motions and documents.

By the end of the afternoon session, the judge's initial *voir dire* questioning of the first twelve prospective jurors was almost completed, and we were optimistic plaintiff's six-day trial estimate might be realistic after all.

Unfortunately, jury selection consumed the entire second day of trial. We learned from the jurors' responses that none of them had slipped or fallen or sued their landlord or property manager. They all seemed to understand the legal concepts of *burden of proof* and *personal responsibility*. I made sure they understood the legal requirement of *notice*, namely, that before a property owner or its agent can be held liable under negligence principles, they must have actual or constructive notice of an unsafe condition and fail to remedy same in a timely fashion.

On the third day of trial, we completed selection of a diverse social, economic, and ethnic group of jurors consisting of seven women and five men, plus one male alternate.

The parties then presented their opening statements, which are intended to act as an outline as to what each side believes their evidence will show. The lead plaintiff attorney was quite dramatic in his presentation and obviously considered himself flamboyant. In his opening statement, he put out a lot of incorrect information we were able to capitalize on in our opening statement and throughout the rest of trial.

The plaintiff's first witness was their safety expert. I requested an *Evidence Code* Section 402 hearing, outside the presence of the jury, to challenge this expert's opinions. Up to this point we had been pleased with the judge's rulings, but over our objection he ruled this expert could opine on the slipperiness of the laundry room floor based *solely* on photographs taken the day after the incident. In my opinion—this was unprecedented.

During cross-examination, I had some fun with this expert. Unbeknownst to the plaintiff and her attorney, the flooring in the laundry room had been replaced a year or two before trial. The attorney sent his expert to the apartment complex to conduct a coefficient-of-friction test on the *new* floor. Because it was not the *same* floor Garcia claimed she slipped on, the test was entirely irrelevant and excluded by the court. I was also successful in exposing the flaws in his opinions. Despite the court's unfavorable ruling on our 402 hearing, this turned out to be a good day for the defense.

On day four of the trial, the plaintiff called her medical expert, who testified Garcia needed neck and back surgery with lifetime medical care. During our cross-examination, the doctor admitted his medical group was treating Garcia on a lien basis and to date she had run up $156,000 in medical bills. Garcia had unlimited free treatment available to her at the nearby

San Bernardino County Medical Center.

Garcia's doctor was forced to admit he had a *financial interest* in the outcome of the trial. If Garcia lost her case, his medical group would not get paid. Therefore, we could argue, and the jurors could infer, this doctor was a biased witness since he had *one-hundred-fifty-six-thousand* reasons to say anything to assist Garcia in winning her case.

The plaintiff also called to the witness stand AVWS's general manager, John Cottrell. Why they called him was unclear and the day ended with plaintiff's lead attorney looking bewildered, and the attorney assisting him, looking upset. The jurors looked bored and the majority were not taking any notes. At this point, Randy's client, AVWS, took their $75,000 settlement offer off the table.

The fifth day of trial started out well for us. One of the female jurors, went into labor over the weekend, was excused, and our male alternate juror took her seat. We now had six men and six women.

The plaintiff continued her case by calling the AVWS tech who replaced a water pump in one of the apartment washers after the alleged incident. He testified credibly that there is no way to know when a water pump is going to fail and no amount of maintenance would have prevented a leak.

Next, Garcia's father, Fausto Sais, speaking through a Spanish interpreter, testified he was visiting from Mexico at the time of the incident, and found Garcia on the floor of the laundry room with a bloody nose. Other than that, he couldn't remember much.

Then, Garcia's husband testified he was not home at the time and didn't inspect the laundry room. He confirmed the property manager came to his apartment the next morning and took a report. He complained that she never followed up, but admitted he was unaware the property was sold a few weeks later, and a new owner and manager took over. When asked why *he* didn't follow up with the property manager, Mr. Garcia replied: "I left that up to my wife to do."

Mr. Garcia also testified on the witness stand, in his opinion, his wife's alleged injuries prevented her from returning to work as a minimum wage, temp employee, and they would now be prevented from buying their "dream house."

Next, Ms. Garcia was on the stand most of the sixth trial day and testified through a Spanish interpreter. Her testimony was impeached multiple times on cross-examination.

The plaintiff's next witness was her former neighbor, Paula Corral, who testified Garcia called her after the incident and requested she come and watch the kids while Garcia went to urgent care. I kept wondering if Corral was going to be Garcia's "smoking gun" witness, but she wasn't. Neither Garcia nor her witnesses testified the property management company had received the requisite prior *notice* of a water leak.

On the seventh trial day, I completed cross-examination of Garcia. In my opinion, she did not make a credible or impressive witness.

Next, her attorney called my client's former property manager, Carla Northup, to the stand. Laboriously, he went over her post-incident interview with Garcia, read portions of the TCPM Policy Manual, and squabbled over whether she took two or four photographs. Carla held her own against some tedious and at times mind-numbing cross-examination. After the defense examined Ms. Northup, Garcia announced she was resting her case.

Both Randy and I made motions for *Non-Suit*,[11] but after consideration, the court denied our motions, stating that although he agreed that the defendant had no *actual* notice, he felt there was some questionable constructive

---

[11] A *Request for Non-Suit* is an option the defense can exercise at the end of the plaintiff's presentation of evidence. If the court finds that the plaintiff has not proven his or her case, the legal action can be terminated.

notice issue for the jury to consider—as to how long the water was on the floor before the plaintiff allegedly slipped. (Per Garcia's testimony—the length of one dryer cycle at best).

The defense then began the presentation of their case-in-chief. I called the apartment's former maintenance supervisor, Jesus Cipres, who backed up Carla Northup's testimony regarding no complaint of any water leak in the laundry room.

After Mr. Cipres, the plaintiff's attorney announced he had an impeachment witness who would testify that the same month as the incident she told Carla there was water on the floor in the laundry room. The problem is the plaintiff attorneys knew about this witness since the first day of trial and rested their case without calling her. This set off a firestorm of argument, and, at first, it appeared that the judge was not going to allow it, but then changed his mind and said he would consider it during the rebuttal phase. He then ordered the Garcia's attorney to immediately provide the witness' contact information to Randy and me.

In the morning session of the eighth day of trial, we called our safety expert Rob Harrison, P.E. (Professional Engineer), who as always, was superb on the witness stand. The plaintiff attorneys were no match for him and finally gave up on their cross-examination. The jurors were all smiles at the end of the day and they would have Mr. Harrison's testimony to think about over the long holiday weekend.

On day nine, Randy conducted the direct examination of our shared medical expert, Dr. Kounang M.D., Director of Rehabilitative Medicine at San Bernardino-Arrowhead Regional Medical Center. Dr. Kounang testified that after conducting a physical examination of Ms. Garcia and reviewing her voluminous medical records, that *only* the initial emergency room, physical therapy and chiropractor treatments could be related to the alleged slip and fall incident. Moreover, he definitively opined that the plaintiff *did not* need future neck or back surgery. Therefore, all the rest of the medical treatment received to date was unnecessary, rendering the $156,000 medical bills—unreasonable.

Next, Randy called three AVWS employees who testified they were at the apartment complex just five days before the incident and observed no water leaking from the washing machines during their inspection. After plaintiff counsel's cross-examination, both defendants rested.

On the tenth day of trial, we finally could see the

light-at-the-end of a very long tunnel. In the morning session, over defense objections, the plaintiff was allowed to call her rebuttal witness. Magdali Lazaro, testifying through a Spanish interpreter, claimed she complained to the office about water on the laundry room floor before the incident date.

On cross-examination, Ms. Lazaro was evasive and combative, refusing to disclose the date and time she complained and a description of the person to whom she supposedly reported the matter. She also refused to provide her husband's name or state her current address. I was prepared and had Carla waiting out in the hallway to rebut Lazaro's testimony.

After Carla's follow up testimony, the evidence phase finally came to an end. The judge then instructed the jury on the law applicable to this case.

Next, Garcia's attorney began presenting his closing argument, which included among other things, a bizarre socialist rant against capitalism and corporate America. It was really quite a performance. He concluded by telling the jurors they should *punish* the defendant corporations by awarding Garcia $970,000 in economic and non-economic damages.

In the afternoon session, Randy presented his closing argument and I concluded with mine. The jury then retired to begin their deliberations.

On the eleventh day of trial, the jury deliberated all day without reaching a verdict. They sent out a question asking if they could see a diagram of the laundry room or visit the scene. The judge, unable to reach the plaintiff attorney by phone, denied their requests.

Finally, on the morning of the twelfth day, the jury completed their deliberations, and rendered the following verdict: "TCPM was found to be twenty percent negligent; AVWS was found to be zero percent negligent; and Garcia was found to be eighty percent negligent."

The jury awarded Garcia total gross damages of $216,297, but after reducing the award by eighty percent, her *net* recovery was $43,297.

Post-trial: After the verdict was read, several jurors hung around to speak to the attorneys in the hallway. They told me that as of the previous day, they were split evenly "six-six." But today, in an effort to move deliberations along and avoid a *hung jury*[12], three jurors compromised on their no liability positions.

At least five jurors told me they *"didn't want to give Garcia a dime,"* but they also didn't want the parties and

---

[12] A *Hung Jury* results where the jury does not have the minimum required number of votes to reach a verdict in a civil case.

attorneys to have to go through a second trial. The jurors who split for Garcia appeared to base their award on peripheral issues, personalities, and emotion, rather than on the facts and the law they took an oath to follow.

Garcia may have won the battle—but lost the war. The cost? Three weeks in trial with not one, but two attorneys, plus the cost of their expert witnesses, and that pesky $156,000 medical lien.

It got even worse for Garcia. Since AVWS obtained a defense verdict, they were entitled to recover not only their trial costs, but also their expert fees. Subsequently, AVWS filed a cost bill for $25,000 against the plaintiff.

For reasons unexplained, Garcia's attorneys failed to *oppose* AVWS' cost bill. This resulted in the court entering a judgment *against* Garcia. Subtracting AVWS' $25,000 cost judgment from the $43,297 net verdict—plaintiff ended up with a final recovery of $18,279.

Consequently, that final figure was all that was left to pay plaintiff's court costs, her trial experts, her medical lien and her two attorneys. In short, Garcia most likely *"didn't recover a dime"* from her lawsuit.

This being my last trial, sure, I would have preferred a defense verdict; but in many ways, this result was even more satisfying. It validated my pre-trial case analysis that Garcia was at least eighty to one hundred percent comparatively negligent.

But most of all, I would have loved to be the proverbial *fly-on-the-wall* when Garcia's attorneys had to explain to her—first, why they didn't accept AVWS' $75,000 settlement offer during the trial—and second, why they didn't oppose AVWS's $25,000 cost bill after trial—which together would have put a $100,000 down payment on Garcia's *dream house*.

Once again, the words of that old tired, but true, legal maxim came to mind: "Pigs get fed, Hogs get slaughtered."

Bibliography

Chapter One:

1. *Connolly v. Webb, et al.,* case number 370267, (Superior Court of Orange County-Santa Ana);
2. *Confidential Report for Attorneys,* 1985, Vol. 18. No. 16;
3. Congratulatory letter from United Pacific Insurance Company dated August 13, 1985.

Chapter Two:

1. *Schaeffer v. Tindall Trucking Company, et al.,* case number N30479, (Superior Court of San Diego County-Vista);
2. *California Lawyer,* June 2011, Discipline Report, p. 45;
3. *Confidential Report for Attorneys,* 1987, Vol.13. No. 20;
4. *Plaintiffs Confidential Report,* August 10, 1987.

Chapter Three:

1. *Bowen v. Kerstin—Laguna Beach, et al.,* case number 400917, (Superior Court of Orange County-Santa Ana);

2. *Confidential Report for Attorneys,* 1988, Vol. 24. No. 17.

Chapter Four:

1. *Martin v. Johnson Trucking Company, et al.,* case number 407196, (Superior Court of Orange County-Newport Beach);

2. *Confidential Report for Attorneys,* 1988, Vol.12. No. 5.

Chapter Five:

1. *Larson v. Loyd, et al.,* case number 543165, (Superior Court of San Diego County-Central);

2. *Confidential Report for Attorneys,* 1989, Vol. 21. No. 18.

Chapter Six:

1. *Myers v. Southern California Edison, et al.,* case number 465842, (Superior Court of Orange County-Santa Ana);

2. *Confidential Report for Attorneys,* April/May 1989;

3. Lichtblau, E., 1989, March 30. "Trial Opens in Suit Arising from Boy's Power-Line Death." *LA Times,* Orange County Section, p. 5; and 1989, April 11. "No

Negligence Verdict for Electrocution Case," *LA Times,* Orange County Section;

4. Zimmerman, J., 1989, March 31. "Edison Faces Lawsuit in Teen's Death." *The Orange Coast Daily Pilot,* pp. A1-A2.

Chapter Seven:

1. *Verstegen v. Phoenix Club, et al.,* case number 444927, (Superior Court of Orange County-Santa Ana);
2. *Confidential Report for Attorneys,* Vol. 27. No. 6.   p. 10. 1990-6;
3. *Plaintiffs Confidential Report,* March 1990, Page 5;
4. Congratulatory letters from the Phoenix Club dated January 31, 1990 and Attorney George Peters dated April 7, 1990.

Chapter Eight:

1. *Lundgren dba CWI Car Co. v. North Carolina Occidental Fire & Casualty Co., et al.,* case number 447913, (Superior Court of Orange County-Santa Ana);
2. *Confidential Report for Attorneys,* Vol. 12. No. 13. 1990. p. 19;
3. *Verdictum Juris,* p. 53, April 1990;
4. Notice of Cancellation of Insurance Policy-Occidental Fire & Casualty Co. of North Carolina;

5. USPS Certificate of Mailing Notice of Cancellation dated August 11, 1983.

Chapter Nine:
1. *Young v. Marcello Trucking, et al.,* case number SOC 75170, (Superior Court of Los Angeles County-Long Beach);
2. *Plaintiffs Confidential Report,* May 7, 1990.

Chapter Ten:
1. *Pate v. Johnson, et al.,* case number 579950, (Superior Court of Orange County-Newport Beach);
2. *Confidential Report for Attorneys,* 1992, No. 1. p. 22;
3. *Plaintiffs Confidential Report,* OR91-11-04, November 1991, p. 5.

Chapter Eleven:
1. *Kiely v. Rooten, et al.,* case number 573141, (Superior Court of Orange County-Santa Ana);
2. *Plaintiffs Confidential Report,* OR91-12-04, December 1991, p. 5.

Chapter Twelve:
1. *Shelat v. Swo-Wei Chai, et al.,* case number 593968, (Superior Court of Orange County-Santa Ana);

2. *Confidential Report for Attorneys*, 1993, No. 16, p. 11.

Chapter Thirteen:

1. *Rollins v. Richardson X-Ray, Inc., et al.*, case number CIV 235534, (Superior Court of Riverside County);
2. *JVR* No. 189597, 1995 WL 907612 (Cal. Super.) (Verdicts & Settlements);
3. *Verdictum Juris*, 1995, p. 11.

Chapter Fourteen:

1. *Wiggins v. Waite, et al.*, case number CIV 281918 Superior Court of Riverside County;
2. *Confidential Report for Attorneys*, April 1999;
3. 17 *Trials Digest*, 3d 94, 1999 WL 318961 (Cal. Super.) (Verdicts & Settlements);
4. *Verdictum Juris*, 1999, p. 11.

Chapter Fifteen:

1. *Montano v. Garcia, et al.*, case number KC029923, (Superior Court of Los Angeles County-Pomona);
2. *Trials Digest Publishing Inc., 33 TD 127*; September 28, 2000, p. 28;
3. Verdicts & Settlements, *Los Angeles Daily Journal*, September 1, 2000, p. 21.

Chapter Sixteen:

1. *Jay/Ransom v. Bechard, et al.*, case number INC 014686, (Superior Court of Riverside County-Indio);
2. *California Jury Verdicts Weekly*, May 2002.

Chapter Seventeen:

1. *Peters v. Lusk, et al.*, case number INC 020133, (Superior Court of Riverside County-Indio);
2. *Plaintiff's Confidential Report*, 04-JV 821, June/July 2004;
3. 26 *Trials Digest* 7th 15, 2004 WL 1460144 (Cal. Super.) (Verdicts & Settlements);
4. *Verdict Search*, May 10, 2004.

Chapter Eighteen:

1. *Ochoa v. Omnitrans Transit Authority, et al.*, case number RCVRS 075105, (Superior Court of San Bernardino County-Rancho Cucamonga);
2. *Trials Digest*, 50 TD 9th 21, December 18, 2006, p. 24;
3. *Verdict Search*, January 22, 2007, p. 12.

Chapter Nineteen:

1. *Adams v. Fernandez, et al.*, case number RCVRS 086322, (Superior Court of San Bernardino County-Rancho Cucamonga);

2. *Verdict Search-California Reporter*, Vol. 7, Issue 6, February 4, 2008, p. 17.

Chapter Twenty:
1. *Glover v. Villa Valencia of Redlands HOA, et al.,* case number CIVDS 1204263, (Superior Court San Bernardino County);
2. 32 *Trials Digest* 16th 24, 2013 WL 4427030 (Cal. Super.) (Verdicts & Settlements);
3. *Verdict Search*, June 3, 2013, p. 10.

Chapter Twenty-One:
1. *Jensen v. Omnitrans Transit Authority, et al.,* case number CIVDS 1108422, (Superior Court of San Bernardino County);
2. *JVR* No. 1404030034, 2013 WL 8284916 (Cal. Super.) (Verdicts & Settlements);
3. *Verdict Search*, January 6, 2014, p. 17.

Chapter Twenty-Two:
1. *Garcia v. JH Real Estate Partners, Inc., et al.,* case number CIVRS 1208628, (Superior Court of San Bernardino County);
2. *Verdict Search*, June 1, 2015, p. 13;
3. Service copy of filed Judgment form;

4. Rough draft cross-examination notes for Dr. Etemad;
5. Trial summary notes;
6. Deposition of Plaintiff's safety expert on CD.

CPSIA information can be obtained
at www.ICGtesting.com
Printed in the USA
BVHW070646311019
562492BV00002B/156/P